Monty at Close Quarters

Monty at Close Quarters

Recollections of the Man

Compiled by

T. E. B. Howarth

Leo Cooper
in association with
Secker & Warburg
London

Hippocrene Books
New York

First published in Great Britain in 1985 by Leo Cooper
in association with Martin Secker & Warburg Ltd,
54 Poland Street, London W1V 3DF

ISBN: 0–436–20170–4

Hippocrene Books, Inc.
171 Madison Avenue
New York, NY 10016

ISBN: 0–87–052–184–5

Printed in England by
Mackays of Chatham

Contents

Introduction

NIGEL HAMILTON'S VERY successful and fair-minded biography, as it winds its majestic way forward, has enabled its
readers to acquire an authentic picture of Montgomery as a
human being which contrasts oddly with much recent writing
about him. Certain marked characteristics of Monty's – his
subordination of all personal considerations to the business of
winning the war; his unconcealed contempt for all whom he
considered to fall seriously short of what was required of
them in war or peace; his vanity and tactlessness; his deeply
ingrained national prejudices – these and other human failings
were bound in the long run to leave his reputation wide open
to detractors. His post-war tendency to claim something
approaching infallibility for the conduct of his campaigns has
particularly irked a number of United States commentators,
both erstwhile colleagues and subsequent military historians.
The accepted wisdom even in this country is epitomised by
a throwaway line in a *Spectator* review by Max Hastings
(2 April, 1983) – "The British Army seemed reluctant to
accept that effective commanders are often ruthlessly unlovely
human beings, Montgomery not least among them."

There was something more to Montgomery than that. In an
earlier biography than Nigel Hamilton's* the late Ronald
Lewin applied to Monty a phrase, originally used to describe
Marlborough – "the power of commanding affection while
communicating energy". Something like that may well lie at
the heart of the secret which enabled him to exercise such a

---

* *Montgomery as Military Commander*, Ronald Lewin, 1971.

strange hold on so many of his contemporaries, from great warlords like Churchill or Alanbrooke to the humble sapper helping to build a Bailey bridge. It would, I think, commend itself as a passably accurate description of what the contributors to this volume, writing from a wide variety of standpoint and background, felt to be their relationship with Monty.

The first three of these short essays were contributed by close and long-standing wartime comrades, Kit Dawnay, Bill Williams and Johnny Henderson. Their recollections and impressions, respectively as Military Assistant, Chief Intelligence Officer and ADC, span between them the campaigns of the BEF, the Eighth Army and 21 Army Group. Like the rest of us they concern themselves with the particularities of Monty's character rather than with the evaluation of his military record. Richard O'Brien and I were for a short period of the war liaison officers at 21 Army Group Tactical Headquarters, but our accounts concentrate for the most part on the post-war period. Mary Soames has, of course, a unique knowledge of the relationship between Monty and the Churchill family both during the war when she was a serving officer and thereafter. Frank Longford picks up the story after the war and describes his friendship with Monty as CIGS while he was a service minister in Attlee's government. Alan Breitmeyer covers Monty's subsequent career in France when he laboured under the strange appellation of Chairman of the Western Union Chiefs of Staff, again from the viewpoint of an ADC. Richard Luckett, Lucien Trueb and Alan Howarth were all in different ways youthful protégés of Monty's (as indeed were Nigel Hamilton and many others). All three of them asked either David Montgomery or myself whether they might contribute and what they have to say has the added immediacy of relatively recent recall. Finally I am greatly indebted to Field-Marshal Lord Harding of Petherton for permission to reprint his memorial address of October, 1977, in the chapel of the Royal Military Academy.

It is inevitable in a work of this sort by a variety of hands that there will be a certain measure of overlap and repetition. However, if the reader derives from that the impression of a character of marked consistency, "all of a piece" as it were, that will not be far from the truth. Colonel Brian Montgomery in his *A Field-Marshal in the Family* recalls a favourite phrase of his brother's: "To find out about a man, his performance and record, you must find out what makes him tick." I am not sure any of us would claim that we knew that, because there was an impenetrability about Monty, but we hope we may have succeeded collectively in throwing some light on many aspects of his character. He was a very unusual human being indeed.

Throughout this enterprise I have enjoyed constant and friendly contact with my old pupil the second Viscount Montgomery of Alamein who has readily given permission for us to use letters and documents which are his copyright. In addition he has been a most helpful source of encouragement, ideas and factual record. The Montgomery Collections Committee and the Trustees of the Imperial War Museum, together with the Director, Dr Alan Borg, gave the project their support and encouragement. I am indebted to Times Newspapers Ltd, for kind permission to print extracts from the Baroness Spencer Churchill Papers. I am grateful also to Sir Denis Hamilton for discussion and advice proferred at a very busy time for him; to Leo Cooper, whose personal knowledge of the subject rendered him a most helpful editor; to Jimmy Beven, formerly Bursar of St John's School, Leatherhead; and finally to Beverley Storkey for the skilful typing of a difficult manuscript.

Notting Hill, 1984

Inside Monty's Headquarters

Kit Dawnay

LT COL C. P. DAWNAY CBE MVO *US Legion of Merit* was born in 1909 and served with the Coldstream Guards. *He was Military Assistant to Montgomery in North-West Europe. A merchant banker, he was Director of Lazard Brothers from 1960–1974 and Chairman of Dalgety from 1963–1977 and of Guardian Royal Exchange Assurance from 1970–1974.*

Even after a lapse of more than forty years I retain a vivid memory of my first encounter with Monty. It took place shortly after the outbreak of war when he inspected our battalion near Warminster. I was at the time thirty years old, a merchant banker by profession and a reservist in my regiment, the Coldstream Guards. I had been posted to the First Battalion which formed part of the Third Division, then commanded by Major-General Montgomery. A great deal had to be done to fit the division for war, since it had never undergone brigade, much less divisional, training. For the first of many subsequent occasions I was an eye-witness of his characteristic method of establishing a personal relationship with the officers and men whom he commanded. He spoke to each officer carefully in turn and then to the whole Battalion. He was shorter than most of the officers but from his piercing blue eyes there emanated such an intensely concentrated gaze that you felt instantly that you were very much on your mettle. He seemed somehow to be probing the depths of your personality – what sort of man were you? Could you be relied on? Would you respond to his leadership? We had none of us met anyone remotely resembling him. It was an uncomfortable experience, but from the outset it induced in me a sense of inspiration and trust which was both immediately stimulating and destined to endure.

By the end of September, 1939, we were in France. The following January I found myself for the first time in close and continuous contact with Monty when I was posted to the divisional headquarters as his GSO III (Intelligence), not selected by Monty but sent by my brigadier. Greatly to my surprise I found myself in his personal mess, comprising just seven or eight officers. Monty always dominated the proceedings at dinner, directing conversation to any topic which currently interested him. Everyone, however junior, was encouraged to express a point of view, provided it was not too laboured, since he had a great loathing of prolixity. Any loose or ill-considered statement would be sharply pounced on – "That's nonsense, my dear fellow!" The subjects discussed were extremely diverse and demanded quick verbal reflexes. It somehow resembled a very fast ball-game in a restricted court with the ball flying all over the place.

In contrast with much that went on elsewhere, Monty kept the Third Division right on its toes during the months of the phoney war. Exercises usually started in the evening and lasted for two or three days. We would move by night with a minimum of illumination, according to an ingenious system devised by his staff, and would "seize" the line of a river by dawn. We would then be "attacked" during daylight hours and after dark would withdraw to another river line to be manned before dawn – and so on till the end of the exercise. This highly realistic training almost exactly prefigured what the division was called on to do once the Germans invaded Belgium. As a consequence, our casualties on the retreat to Dunkirk were, I believe, lighter than those sustained by any other division.

On our return to England we were reformed at Frome and learnt the rather chilling news that we had been selected to re-enter France through Brest, as soon as we could be re-equipped. Monty characteristically decided to visit every unit in the division in the course of one day to inform them of the task ahead together with the highly unwelcome news that no leave would be granted until re-equipment was complete. This must have been the only time that Monty was barracked by some of the troops under his command. On returning to his headquarters he found a message to the effect that although the re-equipment of the division had been ordered it would take longer to effect than he had been led to believe. Without a moment's hesitation and without regard to the serious loss of face entailed, he immediately rescinded the order, which he had only just announced, so that forty-eight hours' leave was granted to all ranks as soon as it could be arranged.

In the event the Third Division did not return to France until four long years later and Monty soon became a Corps Commander. Although I was not destined to serve under him directly again until 1944 he made it very clear that he was not going to forget me. Before he left the division he had asked me to write an appreciation of what steps the Germans would take to develop and exploit their triumph in the Battle of France. I had no access to strategic intelligence but did my best, concluding that there would be an attempt at invasion by 15 August, which I later up-dated to September. I got the following very revealing reply:

20.8.40

My dear Kit,

Thank you for your appreciation. There is no doubt you have the gift of being able to write a clear and easily read memorandum.

I notice in your successive appreciations you keep putting off the date of invasion. If I remember right, No. I said it must come by 15 August, or not at all. Now it is to be in September. I shall ask you again in September – what the real date is!!

I would like to see you again and discuss matters; I have certain ideas on what is likely to happen.

I have hopes I may get you posted here as my G.2(I): I have asked MS* for you and it is now being considered. As you know (or perhaps you don't) I have a very high opinion of your abilities and am trying to take you along with me wherever I go.

* The Military Secretary's department concerned with officers' postings.

Please keep this *entirely* to yourself for the present.

I am afraid I haven't asked you if you want to come with me, and it may be that you would sooner stay with the 3rd Division. Let me know.

Yours ever,

B. L. Montgomery

I was far from being the only young officer in whose training he took a personal interest and would earmark for eventual promotion. Indeed, he kept a little black book to which he confided detailed assessments of the abilities and personal qualities of many officers who thus caught his attention. Nobody ever saw the black book except Monty. Its very colour suggests that not all the biographical data it contained were favourable. It may safely be assumed that Monty's ultimately dismissive epithet "useless" featured at times in its pages.

The following letter reveals Monty hard at work inserting round pegs into what he considered to be round holes:

27.6.41

My dear Kit,

What a dreadful affair about Roger Taverner. He will hate being a prisoner. I am particularly upset as he was one of my "chaps", that I took a special interest in and pushed on up the ladder. Will you send me the address of Mrs Taverner so that I can write to her. I have had you, Bellamy and Tedder earmarked for 12 Corps when you leave the Staff College. MS have been told you are all wanted here and you have been placed on the reserved list.

Yours ever,

Monty

P.S. I have got Horrocks here now, as a Major Gen (sic) commanding 44 Div. This took a bit of doing and is a great triumph. He arrived yesterday.

However, in the circumstances of 1942 Monty's word was not yet law in such matters. His plan to mastermind my military career received a temporary setback when after completing the Staff College course, which he had helped to secure for me, I was posted to the headquarters of what was to become First Army. This meant that we would soon find ourselves at the opposite ends of North Africa. He wrote generously:

5.4.42

My dear Kit,

I am quite delighted that you are going as GSO 1(I) to the Expeditionary Force. But I am desolate at losing you from my Army.* The whole thing is really a complete foul, as they would not let you come to me as GSO 1(I) – saying you were too junior. I gave you such a "write-up" when trying to get you on my staff that they have now bagged you for something else. However, you will find it intensely interesting, and perhaps we may yet fight the Boshe (sic) together again. I hope so.

I hope all goes well with Patsy. Give her my very best wishes.

Yours ever,
Monty

In August, 1942, he was appointed to command 8th Army, and it is interesting to note that he did not take a single one of "his chaps" out with him. He took with him only a junior ADC, but, of course, having served previously in the Middle East, he knew many of the up-and-coming soldiers out there. Shortly after Monty's arrival my father, who had fought in

* Monty had by this time been appointed GOC South Eastern Command, the equivalent of an Army Command.

7

C. P. Dawnay

the First World War, had a letter from "Boom" Trenchard*;
Trenchard had been on a mission to India and stopped in
Egypt on his way out and back. Trenchard's letter – now
unfortunately lost – said more or less: "I have seen an extraordinary situation in Egypt. On my way out I saw a defeated
army with its tail between its legs. On my return a few weeks
later I see the same army rarin' to go. They say a man called
Montgomery has done it."

I, meanwhile, went with 1st Army to North Africa and by
the end of 1942 the Allied forces under Ike were held on a
line some forty miles west of Tunis. Monty by now, having
won the Battle of Alamein and captured Tripoli, was planning
to hold a training conference there, nicknamed "On how to
win the land battle". General Anderson, commanding 1st
Army, was invited to send a few officers to the conference, of
whom I was one. I fortunately met Monty and was at once
invited to dinner, where I was bidden to sit next to him in his
largish mess, where there were also a number of visitors. Then
occurred one of those appalling indiscretions to which Monty
had always been prone, but usually not in front of so large a
number of people. In a sudden lull in the conversation, he
asked me a loud and highly rhetorical question: "Who are
you with now, Kit?" "General Anderson, sir, 1st Army".
"H'm – good plain cook." Observations such as these,
gleefully repeated by his supporters, were calculated to make
him more popular in some quarters than in others. To make
matters worse, the more outrageous they were the more he
enjoyed them.

While Monty's Tripoli conference in February, 1943, was
taking place, Ike in North Africa was holding a long line
from the Mediterranean to the marshes behind Gabes, with
Anderson's 1st Army in the north, the French Corps of
Goums under Koeltz (unmechanized and therefore immobile)
in the centre, and an American Corps in the south. Large

* Marshal of the RAF Viscount Trenchard GCB OM GCVO DSO.

supply dumps of ammunition, petrol and stores were being built up near Tebessa thirty miles behind the southern end of Ike's line for 8th Army's projected advance. The Germans, seeing how extended Ike's dispositions were, attacked in the Kasserine pass area and inflicted a severe defeat on the American troops there. They had never been in action before.

Ike was at his HQ in Algiers, 400 miles away, with no one forward with authority to co-ordinate the defence. Ike asked Anderson on the telephone to send such reserves as he could quickly muster to halt the breakthrough. Anderson acted with speed and ability, and sent a scratch force under his new chief of staff, General Cam Nicholson, who by good generalship halted the German attack. Shortly after, Alexander was appointed land forces commander to co-ordinate the attack on Tunis by 1st Army and 8th Army – a clear recognition that no commander could control the land battle at a distance of 400 miles while also supervising the political and strategical progress of the campaign.

Back again in England after his emotional farewell to 8th Army at Vasto, so movingly described in Nigel Hamilton's book, Monty summoned me to be his Military Assistant, which ensured that I was in daily contact with him for the rest of the war and for some months beyond it. Although deeply involved in the vastly intricate and contentious planning of *Overlord*, he liked to take his mind off strictly military matters by asking a succession of guests from the world outside military planning to lunch or dine with him in his very small mess. His guests were a varied bunch. None was more welcome than his old friend A. P. Herbert. The occasion when Ernie Bevin came to lunch was a brilliant success; Bevin and Monty got on very well together, and understood and appreciated each other. As a general rule Monty liked to start the conversational ball rolling and then sit back and absorb the attitudes and opinions of his guests.

On one occasion I recall Dr Hewlett Johnson, the famous Red Dean of Canterbury, expatiating at great length on the merits of the USSR and the Red Army until Mrs Churchill, unable to bear it any longer, suddenly burst out: "Mr Dean, Mr Dean, you must now listen to me," whereupon she completely silenced him by brilliantly outlining the achievements of Britain and the Allies.

About a month before the invasion Monty, whose personal vanity was markedly not diminished by his new status as the nation's conquering hero, decided that he must have his portrait painted. Since I knew Augustus John slightly I suggested him as the most appropriate artist. John agreed to do a portrait for a very modest fee. After the first sitting my bell rang loudly and I found myself confronted with an outraged Monty – "Kit, who is this terrible man you have sent me to? His clothes are dirty, I think he was rather tight and there are dozens of women in the background. I shan't go again unless you come with me." So I found myself attending all future sittings, where I was usually made to sit in the corner with my face to the wall. This far from cordial atmosphere was considerably lightened during a visit made to the studio one day by Bernard Shaw with whom Monty struck up an immediate rapport. What transpired is described in letters written by Shaw on successive days, later shown to me by the recipient and quoted in Monty's *Memoirs*:

4, Whitehall Court,
London S.W.1
26th February 1944

Dear Augustus John,
This afternoon I had to talk all over the shop to amuse your sitter and keep his mind off the worries of the present actual fighting. And as I could see him with one eye and you with the other – two great men at a glance – I noted the extreme unlikeness between you. You, large, tall, blonde,

were almost massive in contrast with that intensely com-
pacted hank of steel wire, who looked as if you might have
taken him out of your pocket.

A great portrait painter always puts himself as well as his
sitter into his work; and since he cannot see himself as he
paints (as I saw you) there is some danger that he may
substitute himself for his subject in the finished work. Sure
enough, your portrait of B.L.M. immediately reminded me
of your portrait of yourself in the Leicester Gallery. It fills
the canvas, suggesting a large tall man. It does not look at
you, and Monty always does this with intense effect. *He*
concentrates all space into a small spot like a burning glass;
it has practically no space at all; you haven't left room for
any.

Now for it. Take that old petrol rag that wiped out so
many portraits of me (all masterpieces), and rub out this
one until the canvas is blank. Then paint a small figure
looking at you straight from above, as he looked at me
from the dais. Paint him at full length (some foreground in
front of him) leaning forward with his knees bent back
gripping the edge of his campstool, and his expression one
of piercing scrutiny, the eyes unforgettable. The background; the vast totality of desert Africa. Result; a picture
worth £100,000. The present sketch isn't honestly worth
more than the price of your keep while you were painting
it. You really weren't interested in the man.

Don't bother to reply. Just take it or leave it as it strikes
you.

What a nose! And what eyes!

Call the picture INFINITE HORIZONS AND ONE
MAN.

Fancy a soldier being intelligent enough to want to be
painted by you and to talk to me!

Always yours,
(Sgd) GBS

4 Whitehall Court,
London S.W.1
27th February 1944

My dear John,

Having slept on it I perceive that part of my letter of
yesterday must be dismissed as an ebulition [sic] of senile
excitement; for as a matter of business the portrait as it
stands will serve as the regulation one which its buyers
bargained for and are entitled to have (plenty of paint and
the sitter all over the canvas). And between ourselves it has
a subtle and lovely Johannine color plan which must not be
thrown away.

The moral would seem to be to finish the portrait for
your customers and then paint the picture for yourself.
Only, as he certainly won't have time to give you a second
set of sittings you must steal a drawing or two made from
the chair in which I sat.

The worst of being 87–88 is that I never can be quite sure
whether I am talking sense or old man's drivel. I must leave
the judgement to you.

As ever, but doddering,
(Sgd) G Bernard Shaw

Monty's view of the finished article was rather more curtly
dismissive: "Kit, John's picture of me is no good. I am not
going to buy it. You must go and tell him so." This didn't
sound likely to be a very agreeable mission, but I need
not have worried. Augustus John roared with laughter and
immediately pointed out that somebody else would buy the
portrait for much more, which of course turned out to be the
case.

Let me make a brief comment on Monty's so-called vanity.
Monty had always believed it an essential part of "generalship" that a Commander *must* put himself over personally to
the men under his command. During the daytime he was,

whenever possible, visiting troops or to be seen by them – he did not believe in formal inspections if they could be avoided. He set out to build for himself a reputation as a Commander who always won his battles, and did not lose unnecessary lives. Also he was determined to be frequently seen by his troops, and many of them had actually spoken to him. This was to him an essential part of his job – unlike Commanders in the Great War, who were very seldom seen by their troops. His Tank Corps beret with its two badges was part of his *panache* – worth at least an extra Army Corps, as he told George VI. He had a great way with the rank and file and respected them as they respected him. Of the other Commanders in the field, perhaps only Bill Slim had the same sense of the absolute necessity of making personal contact with the fighting troops. It undoubtedly paid off.

After six weeks fighting in Normandy the Allied forces were still pinned down in the *bocage* country. As has been extensively chronicled in so many post-war accounts of the campaign, a considerable chorus of doubt and speculation about Monty's ability to win it began to develop. I had the chance to observe from close quarters that his own confidence never wavered; he knew that he could and would win the battle. However, we had a constant stream of high-ranking visitors to Tac Headquarters who wished to form their own opinion of the prospects of the great battle and of the performance of the land commander. As they came, and went – Churchill, Eden, P. J. Grigg, Alanbrooke, Marshall, Eisenhower, Tedder – all except Tedder were more or less convinced that he would win. The unanswered question was how soon?

To some extent a map which I drew at Monty's direction was partly responsible for the criticism. For his last conference at St Paul's school, attended by all the senior generals, he got me to prepare a map of Normandy showing the beaches and the projected lines of advance up to and including Paris.

This map did not get much exposure, but it was certainly seen by a number of senior commanders and politicians.

The first line I drew covered the beachheads and showed them linked up together. The final line covered the Seine, Paris, and the Loire. I then asked Monty how I should draw the lines in between. "It doesn't matter," he said. "Shall I draw them equally then?" I said. "Yes, that will do," said Monty. I did so, and as a result it appeared to some that Monty had, by D+30 and by D+60, failed to achieve the advance which this map had forecast. By D+90 he had in fact more than achieved the line forecast on the map by that date. Monty's aim throughout the Normandy battle had been to destroy the enemy forces and not to win ground. Once the enemy strength had been destroyed, which he was through-out convinced would be achieved well before D+90, his operational task would be accomplished, and Paris and much other territory would naturally fall into Allied hands.

When at last the great breakthrough came, many Americans naturally chose to give much of the credit to George Patton. Patton indeed much resembled Napoleon's great cavalry leader Murat in his fire and drive, which inspired his troops to advance with great rapidity in fluid conditions. Yet Patton, in fact, was only carrying out the plan which Monty had laid down in England, and furthermore carrying it out to the letter, and Monty had sensed all along that Patton was the right man for this job. American and French troops entered and commenced the liberation of Paris on 25 August – ten days before D+90, as forecast on the map I had drawn for the St Paul's conference.

Monty was also faced with an additional problem during the Normandy battle, which for political reasons was not openly discussed with our allies. England was running short of men, and Monty was told that in the event of heavy casualties it would become necessary to cannibalize some fighting units. Monty was therefore forced to fight the latter part of the battle of Normandy with more caution than he might otherwise have done. Heavy casualties had to be avoided.

The drive forward which liberated Paris, Brussels and much of Belgium brought the Allied forces up to the Rhine in the south but in the north the approaches to Antwerp remained to be cleared, as did pockets on the west bank of the Rhine. And this involved some heavy fighting with not inconsiderable casualties. However, the great sweep forward had encouraged the American high command to think that the war was as good as won, and that one further push *on a broad front* could be successful. And then disaster struck.

During December, 1944, I fear I was to witness an exactly similar error of judgement by Ike to that which he had made in North Africa in February, 1943. He was again over-extended and as a result unbalanced. The German attack through the Ardennes took the Americans by surprise, and they broke through on a wide front towards the Meuse. Ike, from his HQ at Granville on the west coast of the Cotentin peninsula, telephoned Monty to take command of all troops north of the breakthrough which included Ninth and part of Third US Armies, since the Germans had cut their command and supply communications. Monty did as he was ordered. He assigned to 30 Corps under Horrocks the defence of the Meuse bridges, and the American troops in the north under Monty's direction fought most gallantly to restore the situation. In the south the American troops under Bradley by their superb and very brave defence of Bastogne eventually won a costly battle against the German forces. But by this spoiling attack, the Germans undoubtedly delayed the end of the war.

Both these examples showed the need for a land force commander, for which Monty had long campaigned, to co-ordinate the actions of the several army groups – by now almost independent private armies. No one could have controlled them from 400 or 500 miles away. Unluckily Ike would never agree to a land force commander – partly, no doubt, because it would have been difficult to find any individual politically acceptable both to the Americans and their allies.

It was sad, as the campaign went on, to observe the mounting tension between Monty and Ike and the Americans. I was on one occasion, at Monty's request, the only other person in the room when Monty was pressing Ike to agree to the strategy of the narrow-thrust advance into Germany north of the Ruhr. Monty, as always in their discussions, saw the matter in purely military terms – how was the land battle to be won most quickly? Ike, equally inevitably, had to weigh up the political consequences of Monty's tenaciously argued proposal, which he knew would be totally unacceptable to the Americans. In the end Monty's relentless arguments reduced Ike to a condition of speechlessness and he said he was ready for bed. I got him a whisky and soda, escorted him to his room and then came downstairs again. Monty immediately said: "Get this message sent to the C.I.G.S." I wrote it down at his dictation and was astonished to discover that he was claiming that Ike had agreed in general with the single-thrust strategy. I read the message back and asked if it was correct. He assented. I said: "May I say something, sir?" "Yes, certainly." "Ike does *not* agree, sir." His only comment was "Send that message, Kit." And so I did. But Ike had not agreed.

Then, as the race to Hamburg and the Elbe began, Tac Headquarters, which during much of the comparative stalemate of the winter had been relatively static, began to move with ever-increasing speed and frequency. It was always a happy place, full of laughter and high spirits.* I have seen in my life a number of smooth and well-run organizations but none more so than what we affectionately called Tac. But

* We profited greatly from the presence among the team of some friendly Americans and of a particularly delightful Canadian, Trumbull Warren.

for Monty the end of the war, which had culminated in the triumphant surrender ceremony outside his famous map caravan on Luneburg Heath, was much darkened by the death of two of his intrepid young liaison officers, John Poston and Charles Sweeny. They and their comrades had been selected and trained by Monty to be, as he called it, his eyes and ears. They were sent out daily to wherever the battle was fiercest to bring back detailed reports to the caravan every evening. As a result, Monty was kept in continuously close touch by eyewitness accounts with the fighting as it took place and so could intervene and influence the battle as he saw fit. John Poston had been with him since Alamein and Monty was greatly attached to him. He had known Charles Sweeny even longer and felt impelled to send a very revealing obituary of him to *The Times*, which reads as follows:

Major Charles Sweeny MC

It is with a heavy heart that I record the death of another member of my team of liaison officers, who was also a former ADC – Charles Sweeny of the Royal Ulster Rifles. It is a tragedy that of that team of gallant young LO's whose photograph appeared in the Illustrated London News of 5th May, two are now dead (John Poston and Charles Sweeny) and one is lying wounded in hospital in Germany (Peter Earle). The photograph was taken on 12th April.

The loss of Charles is hard to bear. I first got to know him in Palestine in the troublesome days of the winter of 1938/39 when the 2nd Battalion RUR was serving in that country; later his battalion was in the 3rd Division, which I took to France in September, 1939, and it was in those days that began my close association with him. He became my ADC early in 1940, and was with me in the Dunkirk days. Charles was an orphan and possibly it was that fact which drew us close together; he knew the depth of my devotion to him because I had told him of it; he knew that he could call on me for anything he needed, as if I was his father.

He was an Irish boy with a delightful brogue. There was nothing he liked more than a good argument; he would "trail his coat" with great skill and, when discussion was started, he would take whichever side was likely to lead to the most heated argument; nothing would shake him from his adopted line of country.

He had a very strong character and was utterly incapable of any mean or underhand action; his sense of duty was highly developed, and his personal bravery very great. His death is the more tragic in that the road accident which led to it occurred after the German surrender on the north flank had taken place; he was escorting a German Admiral back to Kiel and the car left the road and crashed into a tree.

I loved this gallant Irish boy and his memory will remain with me for all time.

B. L. Montgomery
Field-Marshal

Summing up my memories of Tac, I am inclined above all else to stress the fact that one always had the curious feeling of being *taught* – and by a great master. In this connection it is interesting to note that he was privately and affectionately known by those who worked for him at 8th Army Tac HQ as "Master". There were always new things to be learnt from him. What I myself learnt proved of inestimable value throughout my subsequent business career. It was a quite unforgettable experience.

Gee One Eye, Sir –

Experiences of an Intelligence Officer

Bill Williams

A son of the manse, Sir EDGAR WILLIAMS CB, CBE, DSO, DL, was born in 1912 and served as a subaltern with the King's Dragoon Guards in an armoured car in the Western Desert, where he was the first to bump by chance into the Afrika Korps on 20 February, 1941. As successively GSO2, then GSO1 8th Army, and Brigadier, General Staff (Intelligence) 21 Army Group, he was Chief Intelligence Officer to Montgomery from 1942–1946. After the war he worked in the secretariat of the United Nations Security Council until 1947 when he returned to Oxford where he was a Fellow of Balliol College from 1945–1980. He was Secretary of the Rhodes Trust from 1951–1980 and Editor from 1949–1980 of the Dictionary of National Biography *(in which he has written both the notice of Churchill (1981) and that of Montgomery in the forthcoming supplement).*

W<small>HAT WAS IT</small> like to serve on General Montgomery's staff now more than forty years ago?*

My own experience was far from typical, since my job was to tell him about the enemy facing him so that I was licensed, so to speak, to contradict him. And that, I suppose, is scarcely typical of anyone's relationship with Generals, that one especially. Also, I was particularly fortunate in that "Freddie" de Guingand whom he had inherited from Wavell and Auchinleck, and made his Chief of Staff, had been Director of Military Intelligence in Cairo from 1941: so I had already worked, enthralled, under him. Freddie de Guingand was the best man I've ever worked for anywhere (save later in peacetime when I joined the Rhodes Trust and worked under Sir Edward Peacock, a very much older man).

Not long after General Montgomery's electrifying arrival at HQ 8th Army, I was told he wanted to see me. I was summoned to the caravan pretty early on, 15 or 16 August, 1942, perhaps. (I couldn't keep a diary, because of the vital security of "Ultra").

The new Army Commander had uncomfortably piercing eyes which also seemed to be hooded, a disconcerting

---

* Part of the original version of this slight personal footnote to history appeared in *The Times* on the day after the Field-Marshal's death in late March, 1976, and was first written before "Ultra" had been unveiled (in 1974) or the appearance of Nigel Hamilton's *Monty* (vol i 1981; vol ii 1983). I have not myself ever seen the Montgomery Papers themselves in their vast entirety.

combination. He listened with his whole frame vibrantly still, never interrupting. His questions in a sharp, spinsterly voice were directly on target. He wanted to know when "Rommel" would attack, where and what with. General Montgomery had already begun to personify Rommel as the enemy. Indeed, he had inherited the personification, like much else. We had all referred to the enemy, the Axis forces, as "Rommel" for quite a while already. Monty soon saw the convenience of that to himself. Incidentally, we didn't call him Monty; obviously not to his face, but not even behind his back. He was either "the Army Commander" or "Master", the name the ADCs used on the field telephone.

But I'm interrupting. As I have just said, the Army Commander wanted to know three things – the time, the place and the scale of the enemy attack. More interestingly, it was not three but four. He devoted most of his time that first morning I spent with him (I had barely become a major and was I think, still wearing three pips) interrogating me about the enemy defences at Alamein. The new Commander of Eighth Army was one battle ahead of the rest of us. Lieutenant-General Montgomery was already devising the offensive which was to make his name.

The answers to the first three queries were reasonably clear; in fact, as clear as the desert daylight. It so happened that almost never before and rarely ever again did we have evidence so hard and cold and up-to-date as to be able to give any Commander a pretty precise answer. It was a fluke – a fluke, admittedly, in which a lot of hard work was involved, of which I was merely the mouthpiece that morning. Well, that was fine: but he had only just arrived and why should he believe us? Well, he did. And this established a relationship. He won his first battle, the model defensive battle of Alam Halfa, by believing in the Intelligence with which he was furnished that morning. From that tight-reined success at

Alam Halfa sprang the morale needed for victory at Alamein not too many weeks later.

It meant, too, that because the Intelligence had proved adequate then, he believed it thereafter – not gratefully (I doubt if gratitude was in his make-up) but practically – in practice. Moreover, thereafter it was *his* Intelligence and that curious anxiety to absorb everything unto himself, that dominating, I had almost said frenetic, possessiveness, meant that, because *he* was never wrong, *his* Intelligence couldn't be wrong either. Neither of these flattering propositions was, of course, true, but, as rough-and-ready assumptions, they worked, by-and-large, as the months passed. But why he believed it all so readily the first time I've sometimes wondered. "Ultra" was a dazzling new experience, heady medicine for any General and Montgomery's self-confidence, as its newest legatee, was to become its most effective cover. "Alone I done it", which was his life style, protected Ultra better than the rest of us could have invented in front of any mirror.

Mind you, there were difficulties. Military Intelligence is not only spasmodic, it is always out of date: there is a built-in time-lag. Better the half-truth on time than the whole truth too late. (Not a recipe for the historian but vital to the Intelligence officer). So that, although, to be useful to a commander, it must provide as clear an answer as possible (not just a set of possibilities in no order of probability, which he himself can pick and choose between). One more clue can readily refute it. It follows, therefore, that one complete irrelevance to Military Intelligence is vanity. Going on believing that the picture carefully confected from a wealth (it is more often from a paucity) of detail, is still true when it isn't raises hideous problems. Men are being killed because of your false information.

This became an especial problem in the case of General Montgomery. He liked his enemy simplified (though he was more interested in the details than he pretended, because he loved gossip of all kinds, whatever his self-delusions). It became a difficult note to strike because one knew that he himself would simplify the story still further and that he didn't like being wrong: not that I remember that he ever tried to visualise such a notion.

So that, whereas vanity was part of his impetus – and his vanity was part of Eighth Army's morale, indeed its dynamo – non-vanity about being wrong was doubly essential to his Intelligence service. And I think that my having begun before the war to become a history don helped in this.

Don't mistake me. I am not pretending that dons aren't as vain as the next man, certainly not after more than fifty years in Oxford, I'm not. I mean only that, as a tribe, they can't bear something wrong to go on being believed and, if you will, one aspect of their sort of vanity consists of getting it right, or seeing that other people get it right or (especially) not allowing other people to remain wrong.

In his own sort of way – and he couldn't not simplify everything – General Montgomery cottoned on to this. The "Q" chaps, say, were rebukable if they didn't have enough of whatever was wanted, although I am certain that he never questioned the highly professional opinion of either "Sir B" (Brian Robertson) or Miles Graham, whereas the "I" chaps, by contrast, gave him the likeliest answer they could for that moment and corrections were therefore the latest (although it must be always out-of-date) available information. I think too, looking back, that being regarded as a don in uniform helped the relationship. He didn't expect a don (again he simplified, for in those days I was only a Junior Research Fellow of Merton) to talk to him in quite the same way as the others did and because the don was supposed to be representing the enemy, anyway; secondly, I think that when Montgomery came to compose his circus, it amused him to maintain that, in his case, he always had an Oxford don as his "Intelligence chap". He just didn't want to know that the desert, and lots of other places, were cluttered, like old thoughts, with dons involved in Intelligence work of one sort or another: David Hunt with General "Alex", for instance, just up the track there.* No, no, Montgomery's staff had to be unique.

Unique or not, it was certainly very hard work. As time went on we ("my Intelligence chaps") were less used, I think. You don't need Intelligence quite so badly when you are winning – although it can still come in pretty useful if you want – as he always did – to do it more economically. At Medenine, of course, the Intelligence dictated the timing; but in Sicily, our first "away match", no, not really. For D-Day in Normandy, yes, indeed; but after the battle in France, not a great deal, I think, as I look back. And we were wrong about the Ardennes anyway, although quick Intelligence (not mine) enabled Montgomery to react more rapidly than most. And I don't myself believe that the Arnhem operation would have gone much better had the Intelligence been first class, and it was very far from that, certainly in my case. I am sure that he had decided to get his hands on those "spare" airborne divisions and swing the *Schwerpunkt* north-east, whatever information we had provided, or however dubious Oliver Poole and I, or anybody else, might have been about the utility of that particular operation.

So, there were times when I saw quite a lot of him, times when our contacts were more perfunctory. Partly this was because the theatre expanded. He had his small Tac HQ and I worked, because of the nature of my job, from Main HQ. My friend "Joe" Ewart, who was killed with Private Currell, my driver, the day after the war ended in Europe, was my half-section as the "I" chap at Tac. Partly, I think,

* His *A Don at War* (1966) is for me the most satisfying account I know of those far off desert days.

the Army Group Commander became less interested in the enemy *per se* after Rommel disappeared from the scene. Moreover, his own command level had shifted, so he needed Intelligence at a different enemy level too; not so obviously minute by minute as in the days when I had seen him well before breakfast in Africa and Italy.

When we heard on the BBC, about Christmastime, 1943, that he had been appointed to what we called "the Second Front", we were on the Sangro. I went up to Tac early on Boxing Day morning with Currell. "If the Army Commander takes me back with him," I told him en route, "I'll see to it that you get home too."

The enemy were spending a quietish Christmas on their side of the river and the only information I had of interest for my Commander for that morning's breakfast was not about them but that I had gathered that General Freyberg was proposing to swim the river that night and that it might perhaps be a good idea to stop him. "I've got good news for you, Bill," said the Army Commander. My heart jumped. "Here it comes," I thought. "Yes," he went on, "I remembered that you and Mr Harwood (his clerk) both smoke pipes; so I have been saving this tin of tobacco for you for Christmas." I thanked him slightly less than warmly, saluted after my fashion and went down the steps of the caravan to Currell's expectant face. We drove back in a loud sheepish silence to my truck at Main HQ, where Corporal Young, the clerk, was waiting impatiently. "ADC on the line, sir," he said. "What is it, Johnny?" I asked Johnny Henderson. "I've only just left the little so-and-so." "Well, he wants to talk to you." "Gee One Eye* here, sir" I reported. "Is that you, Bill?" came that familiar high-pitched voice: "Army Commander speakin'. I forgot to tell you that I'm taking you back to England with me.

* The abbreviation for General Staff Officer, Grade One, Intelligence – a Lieutenant-Colonel's appointment.

D'you want to come?" (Currell arrived in England a few days later).

There were obvious advantages, and no obvious disadvantages I can think of, in direct access. It was always intensely interesting; it was not invariably enjoyable, just as it was certainly never really disagreeable. It was very important not only to tell him when one was wrong about the enemy but also to avoid loitering out of the territory of one's own pretended expertise; and most assuredly, if one was so loitering, then never without first clearing the position with the Chief of Staff, who admittedly might sometimes find it a slight advantage to have a far more junior officer advance an awkward suggestion (like the change in the thrust line, [*Supercharge*] at Alamein). During the tension about the change of command after Normandy, it was convenient to be able to take the opportunity to indicate to the Army Group Commander when pressed by him that, even if the Americans thought him the best General in the world and this, one might shyly suggest, was a doubtful proposition, he still wouldn't be invited to remain the Ground Force Commander when our armies were shrinking and theirs' still growing daily. This seemed at the time to strike him as a strange idea – and perhaps represented the enemy point of view. Again, in Brussels, after addressing the Staff in some smokeless cinema or other, he went on to talk of the post-war world. Since half the staff seemed to be waiting to be elected to the House of Commons, this part of the address was bitterly resented by some; and I was told by Freddie that it wouldn't do any harm if I let "Master" know in the course of a routine session on another item. "After all, you're a civilian," he said. Fortunately, "Master" raised the matter himself. So I explained that, whereas we would all follow him to the death till the war ended – there wasn't much option, anyway – nevertheless, we reserved the privacy of our own post-war. "You'll remember Wellington's windows, sir," I ventured. No, he didn't.

"Well, sir, the fact that the Duke of Wellington won the Battle of Waterloo, just down the road, didn't stop his windows being stoned when he turned politician." He sent a charming note to Freddie to let the Staff know that he was sorry to have given the impression of having trodden on their post-war corns.

Did I like him personally? Yes, I did; I liked him very much indeed. He was an exhilarating experience, as the rest of Eighth Army had soon discovered. One was impressed by his sheer competence, his economy, his clarity, above all by his decisiveness. He had made himself the complete professional and he was therefore a quite admirable man to discuss the enemy with, for the Germans, as soldiers, were nothing if not highly professional too. Given such temporary facts as I might muster by breakfast-time, his appreciation of what they might add up to was always invigoratingly well worth arguing with and made one pick one's own brains better too. He was a high-spirited character most of the time (though he could have his shrouded moods), indiscreet, vivid, and, if his humour was perhaps not infrequently barely banana skin deep, it reflected a resolute, betimes insensitively arrogant, self-confidence which was quickly transmitted and buoyed up one's own spirits far from home. Fearless, often ruthless, even baleful in opinion, he was also physically extremely brave, even for a regular soldier. And all my life I have admired physical courage. To my dying day (which seemed at the time to be at that very moment), I shall never forget the nonchalance of those knobbly knees, the unbroken flatness of the unemphatic tones of the Army Commander when a solitary freak Messerschmitt zooped down on us, machine-guns throbbing, as we were taking a peek at the Mareth Line a day or so after I had come out of hospital at Tripoli – and now seemed likely to go back there or elsewhere any second. Corsetted by his conscious imperturbability, one was too afraid to be afraid. (Johnny Henderson tells a similar story from about the same period about when they went together to visit the Guards Brigade.)

Neither then nor later did I ever have a cross word from him. He never tore a strip off me. He listened intently; he gave one his entire, almost fiercely concentrated, attention. Remembering now, I marvel that so authoritarian, so hierarchical a character should have taken so much lip from me, whatever its phrasing or the topic. Swift to contemn the established – "Brookie" (the CIGS, his surrogate conscience) stood alone, I would suppose, in being yielded General Montgomery's undiluted respect – he was always kind, indulgent to the young whom he had picked or inherited; and I was a very unseasoned twenty-nine year old when he first arrived in the Western Desert in August, 1942. (I had left England for North Africa with my regiment, the King's Dragoon Guards, in 1940). So, in the privileged point of vantage which I have depicted, it is hardly surprising that I should have found General Montgomery a very good man to serve. He trusted me, which was flattering. Of course, there were bits of him I didn't very much like. His idea of fairness, and more particularly of truth, did not always march in step with mine, would sometimes chill me inside and worry me, perhaps unduly. I uncovered this to myself all over again long after the war when I was down at the Mill at Isington in 1957–8 helping him with his *Memoirs*. But they are very much Montgomery's memoirs: assuredly, they are not mine: accordingly, they have Montgomery's highly personal flavour (even, I would claim, to the self-analysis at page 111 which, incidentally I happened to supply for him). Peacock pie is scarcely the same as steak-and-kidney pudding, after all.

As I have said, he was a pro. And he treated me as if I were a pro too, in terms of my stuff and what I was supposed to know about. And, as I look back now in 1984, I am realizing all over again how often how little I really did know about it all then, and how, time and time again one was rescued by others, by the fertile brilliance of Freddie de Guingand, and by the scholarly ingenuities of Joe Ewart, of David Hinks, and of John Simmons, as well as all those other dons and their wartime colleagues afar off in Bletchley with whom we were in nightly communion.

As Nigel Hamilton steadily unveils the Montgomery Papers for us, we are beginning to see the strange old Field-Marshal more clearly across the years between. There have been plenty of backbiters, as indeed there were when his own bite was still tangible. One of the fairest epitomes I have run across myself was by Brigadier C. J. C. Malony who died, alas, before I had the chance to meet him, who generously swallowed his distaste in his admirable *Official History*: *The Mediterranean and Middle East* Vol V(1973) at pp. 510–513. And another official historian, Professor Michael Howard, has given us an unofficial opinion which I happen, in general, to share in his *Causes of Wars* (1983) at pp. 208–233. Myself, although military history is far from being my own main interest (or his either, I would suppose) I would readily go along with Mr A. J. P. Taylor's assertion, at p. 557, in his enjoyably idiosyncratic volume of the Oxford History: *English History 1914–45* (1965): "Montgomery was the best British field-commander since Wellington."

And while you have Mr. Taylor's sturdy volume to hand, let me polish off this prejudiced footnote by citing two sentences from p. 508: "Montgomery had a university teacher, E. T. Williams, as his chief Intelligence officer. Of course many mistakes were made."

Morning, Noon and Night
the story of an ADC

Johnny Henderson

J. R. HENDERSON MBE *was born in 1920 and served with the 12th Royal Lancers. He was ADC to Montgomery from 1942–1946. He was a senior partner of the stockbroking firm of Cazenove and Co. He is a Director of Barclay's Bank and Chairman of Barclay's Trust Company and of Henderson Administration Group. He is Chairman of Racehorse Holdings Trust which owns eight racecourses including Cheltenham, Newmarket, Haydock and Liverpool and on behalf of the Jockey Club carried out the recent negotiations which secured the future of the Grand National. He was responsible for the erection of the statue of Montgomery by Oscar Nemon in Whitehall.*

I was TWENTY-TWO years old and a Second Lieutenant in the 12th Royal Lancers which was an Armoured Car Regiment that had come out to Egypt in 1941. I had had one year's fighting up and down the desert before the battle of Alamein and it was a week after the breakthrough there that I was told by my Colonel, George Kidston, that I was to go and be ADC to the new Army Commander. If I didn't like the job after a fortnight I could return to my regiment. If he didn't like me, I certainly would.

So with some trepidation I set off, appreciating as never before the company of my soldier servant, to the newly established Tac Headquarters, not remotely imagining that this was the prelude to four and a half years, during which I would have breakfast, lunch, tea and dinner with Monty almost every day. I knew that there would be one friendly face to greet me as I was already acquainted with the other ADC John Poston, a captain in the 11th Hussars. But up to that point I do not suppose I had ever talked to a General in the field, much less an Army Commander.

In the event my fears were groundless. I remember being somewhat surprised by the informality and friendliness which prevailed throughout this small headquarters. Although I had two or three minutes with Monty before dinner, it was not until we had sat down that I was exposed to the characteristic interrogation – Where had I been to school? Where did I live? Was I any good at anything? I was immediately helped by the friendly way I was put at my ease by the Chief of Staff,

Freddie de Guingand, little imagining the countless evenings I would spend with him in the future playing cards till the small hours.

I shared a tent, let down from the side of Monty's caravan, with John Poston until after the campaign in Sicily and we became close friends. He was only twenty-three but already knew his way round the desert with supreme confidence. In the early days it was John whom Monty sent off to Corps, Division, Brigade or even Battalion headquarters to find out exactly what was happening and that was no easy job in the mobile conditions of an advance in the desert. John's success in bringing back first-hand information was the forerunner of Monty's later employment of liaison officers.

John enjoyed living dangerously, but only once did a joint escapade on our part threaten disastrous consequences. The night before Winston came to Tripoli we thought we would visit the local night club for an hour or two and rather foolishly took Monty's open Humber – the only proper car at Tac and the one in which Monty was to take Winston around the next day. We came out about 2 a.m. to find to our horror that the car had been stolen. After a moment's mutual bewilderment, John took the situation in hand. We got a lift to the Military Police headquarters. When we arrived there about 2.30 we explained our dilemma and they immediately got as many military policemen on the job as they could while we waited. Luckily the car was soon spotted weaving down a road leaving Tripoli with a drunken soldier at the wheel. We managed a couple of hours' sleep before the big day.

All who served at Tac HQ owe John Poston a great debt for establishing the principle that, confronted with Monty, whatever one's rank as an officer, one always said exactly what one thought. But even he, as a regular soldier, found it difficult to tell Monty that he wanted to leave the Army after the war. As a result he was sent somewhat unwillingly to the

Staff College, returning to us as a Liaison Officer just before the Normandy landing. About a month after that he told me that he was violently in love and regretted having left England without proposing. Might not somebody else slip in and what should he do? After a good many whiskies we decided that the best chance was for him to tell Monty and ask if he could have some leave. The plan worked, Monty saying immediately: "Take my aeroplane and go back to England for three or four days, but you must clear this mess up one way or another. No good having you moping around like this." John came back three days later, still unattached. Towards the end of April, 1945, he was ambushed and killed on his way back from Lüneburg, a few miles from Tac HQ at Soltau. Monty's intense grief as he led a small procession to a meadow near the caravans where John was buried was palpable, though he said little.

John had been succeeded as my fellow ADC by Noel Chavasse, son of the Bishop of Rochester, an old friend of Monty's. He soon got the hang of working for Monty, acting nearly as quickly as he talked and very much became part of the team. It was Noel who set up Monty's personal side of the Tac HQ in France on the Normandy landing, while I had the more enviable job of leaving Portsmouth with him on the night after D-Day on HMS *Falkner*. The unflappable side of Monty's character was highlighted when next morning, on board the ship, I went to tell him what news we had of the progress of the landing, but also had to tell him that the captain had just said we had lost the swept channel some hours before and had "hoved to" (or whatever the naval expression is). He came up on board with a chirpy "Lost, lost are we?" and was even less perturbed when action stations were called for as a battleship had been sighted. It turned out to be American and we had been swept down off the Cherbourg Peninsula.

*

Monty's habits in the desert and thereafter were simple and regular. He would be called by his soldier servant, Corporal English, at 6.30 every morning with a cup of tea and would not come out of his caravan till 8 to walk across to the mess tent for breakfast. You could set your watch by his regular visit to the WC. He would retire to bed at 9.30 in the evening no matter who was visiting the headquarters. Even when George VI came he would say: "If you will excuse me, Sir, we have the battle to win and I must go to bed. These lads will sit up all night drinking and I trust they will look after you." He went to bed as usual at 9.30 on the eve of the Normandy landing, saying: "Come and tell me the news at 6 a.m." He was awake when I went in and just said quietly, "What's the news?"

Living conditions were sometimes quite spartan. In southern Italy we were once in a very primitive house. As I walked down the passage I noticed Monty trying to have a bath where there was no running water. He was calling out to Corporal English to bring him some cold water. Noticing a jerry can in the passage which I presumed to be full of water, I opened the door to come to the rescue. He was standing up in the bath lifting his feet in and out of the very hot water. He took the can and poured what turned out to be Marsala wine over a vulnerable area above the knees. He was not at that moment as amused as I was, but afterwards frequently enjoyed telling the story of how I was unable to tell the difference between wine and water.

Dinner in the evening was the only period of relaxation. In the desert there were often not more than three or four of us, though there would be a greater number in Europe. Nearly every night he would provoke a conversation, often of a trivial, bantering nature, which would often run something like this:

Monty: "Johnny, have you read my latest pamphlet on military training?"

Reply: "No, matter of fact I haven't."

Monty: "Well, you will never make a soldier if you don't get down to that."

Reply: "But I don't want to be a soldier."

Monty: "Alright, what do you want to do?"

Reply: "I don't really know, but perhaps I might go into the City."

Monty: "Oh, you want to make money, do you? That won't do you any good. Anyhow, it's no good saying 'You don't know' – you had better make up your mind."

One evening in Belgium he sat down and asked us for our definition of a gentleman. He clearly thought we weren't doing very well, as indeed we weren't, so he said: "Well, we'll ask Winston when he comes out next week." On Winston's first night we had not been sitting down long before Monty duly remarked: "I have been asking these fellows for a definition of a gentleman and they aren't very good at it – what's yours?" Winston thought for a moment and said: "I know one when I see one," and then added: "I suppose one might say – someone who is only rude intentionally."

Monty had a good sense of humour and could tell a story really well, often against himself. He enjoyed recounting a story which dated from pre-war days when he was commanding a battalion of the Royal Warwickshire Regiment in Egypt. One of his young officers was, in Monty's view, doing himself no good by being out too often with the girls. "So I gave him an order not to have another woman without my permission, though if I thought it necessary I would give it." Some weeks later he was dining in Cairo with the Ambassador, Lord Killearn. During the dinner the butler announced that there was a telephone call for Colonel Montgomery. The

Ambassador said: "Ask who it is and what he wants." The butler returned and gravely announced: "It is Lieutenant X and he wants to ask the Colonel if he can have a woman." Permission was granted.

But life for the most part was, of course, deadly serious and it was only at dinner that there was any conversation apart from the task in hand. In the desert one always drove him and he would sit, silent and brooding, in the front seat alongside. During the innumerable hours I spent in this way I can hardly recall him ever saying a word and it was certainly not one's place to start chattering. One could occasionally sense when he was worried because he was inclined then to be snappy. However, the moment we arrived at a particular headquarters – Corps, Division, Regiment or Battalion – he would alight as if he hadn't a care in the world. He would ask straightaway what was going on and radiate the most amazing sense of confidence. His extraordinary capacity to inspire confidence in this sort of way was riveting. He made a practice always on these occasions of putting the headquarters which he was visiting "into the bigger picture", which was both flattering and helpful in building up a sense of unity throughout the whole army. He was also remarkably unruffled when things went unavoidably wrong. If arrangements had to be altered because of adverse flying conditions or because some visitor might be delayed he would just accept the situation. We heard not a word of complaint, for instance, when one evening in the desert the mess tent was blown down with consequences which can be imagined.

As is well known, he liked familiar faces round him and by putting his faith in people in the way he did he got the best back from them in return. Above all, he put his trust in Freddie de Guingand and Bill Williams. In my opinion he relied on Bill's judgement in the field more than on anyone else's. Much has correctly been written about the qualities of Generals Dempsey, Leese and Horrocks, who were his favourite subordinate commanders. Every day he would be in close personal contact with one or all of them. Theirs was a comradeship of mutual trust and confidence. He liked to see enthusiasm, courage and a spirit of adventure – and funnily enough "good manners". He disliked anyone who complained or made excuses and would constantly describe such a person as "a belly-acher". He liked people to speak up fearlessly and the fact that this was naturally easier for non-regulars may account for the fact that he had so many around him. He trusted us implicitly and felt that there was more security in telling us what was going to happen – e.g. the date of D-Day – than in leaving us guessing. He treated his three chosen war reporters, Alan Moorehead, Alex Clifford and Christopher Buckley, in much the same way. He told them in advance his battle plans and trusted them to lead the press and not let him down and they didn't.

Yet, despite all this, one never really got close to him. He didn't let anyone do that in the sense that no one had the right to impose on his inner life. In all those years I never heard him mention his wife. When he talked about his son, David, it would be in connection with the planning of his holidays rather than from the viewpoint of an affectionate father. He was served magnificently by his personal soldier servant, Corporal English, and by his drivers, particularly Sergeant Parker, who stayed with him after he left the Army. But he would never start a conversation with them, and they knew never to start a conversation with him.

There seems to have grown up a belief that he was religious. He certainly had a bible by his bed at all times and went to church whenever the opportunity arose. Undoubtedly he was a believer and an upholder of the Christian religion, but it was a matter which he kept to himself and although many subjects were discussed in the evenings at dinner, religion was never one. However, whenever it was possible in the desert on a Sunday he would summon up the Chaplain-General Padre Hughes who would conduct a service for us.

It is interesting to recall in what ways Monty altered during the four years I was with him. From the time of his short visit to England after Tripoli, when he was idolized wherever he went to a quite unbelievable extent, he was always in the limelight and this he enjoyed more and more. With the increased publicity went what amounted to a growing obsession that he must always be right. It was significant that in the early period in the desert he would write up his diary each evening to cover the day's happenings, whereas later he would leave it for three or four days, thus giving himself a chance to be wise both before and after the event. A reflection of his overweening self-confidence was the curtly dismissive way in which he would write off other prominent figures. "Jumbo" Wilson was "useless – useless"; Anderson "no more than a plain cook"; Mountbatten "wouldn't trust him – wouldn't want to be in the jungle with him". Eisenhower, whom he undoubtedly liked tremendously as a person, usually aroused the comment: "no fighting soldier – political soldier, yes, but doesn't know how to fight a battle". However, as late as December, 1946, when Monty took me with him to stay with Ike in his home outside Washington it was clear that they still much enjoyed each other's company, Monty greatly appreciating Ike's remarkably extensive knowledge of British military history.

His relationship with Alexander was always friendly, indeed genial. This was thanks totally to Alexander's policy of leaving him alone to fight the battles, while supporting him in every way. Alexander very seldom came to 8th Army headquarters. This suited Monty fine. He rarely criticized Alex openly, although it was obvious that he considered him incapable of making a decision when it came to a difficult problem.

Yet there were those whom he particularly admired, especially, as is well known, Alanbrooke. Indeed I would say that Alanbrooke was the only person of whom Monty stood

in awe. He knew he owed his job to him more than to anyone else. He not only always listened to him but would
accept admonishment from him without protest. Only for
Alanbrooke would Monty concern himself with the detailed
arrangements prior to a visit. His relationship with Churchill
and his family meant of course a very great deal to him and he
was fascinated by Smuts. His respect for Attlee grew rapidly.
He almost ignored him at the start of the Potsdam Conference, but when Attlee returned to the Conference as Prime
Minister Monty soon learned to respect his judgement. After
the war and before he became CIGS he suggested to Attlee
that he, Monty, would be the right person to run the coal-
mines, an idea based on his admiration of the 50th (Tyne and
Tees) Division. Attlee did not agree. Apart from his old friend
A. P. Herbert whose visits to Tac were always hilarious,
Monty was closest to P. J. Grigg, Secretary of State for War
from the time of the Normandy landing, a shy, clever man,
who would read the *Confessions of St Augustine* while flying
over to Tac. Grigg used to spend Christmas with him at
Isington Mill after the war, and a really warm friendship
developed between them.

Monty also enjoyed the company of Colonel Jack Gannon,
Military Secretary to 21 Army Group, a gentle, rather old-
fashioned and wholly delightful Indian cavalry soldier. Since
the Military Secretary is responsible for officer appointments
his was a key appointment as far as Monty was concerned,
nothing being more important in his eyes than the character
and quality of his commanders and staff officers. He took
infinite trouble with all appointments down to the level of
commanding officers of regiments and battalions. In the
desert the Military Secretary was "Shrimp" Coghill, who was
a constant visitor to the caravan as was Gannon in the days of
21 Army Group. There was no truth in the idea put about
that Monty disliked the cavalry and the Guards – rather,
he wanted to get them behind him and didn't know how.

However, he would pull Jack Gannon's leg by regaling him with his celebrated list of cavalry officers' priorities in life on service in India, their diaries on arrival filled with dates of polo tournaments, racing, pig-sticking and cocktail parties, a discourse which invariably concluded with the remark: "No wonder there are no good cavalry soldiers".

The obsession for always being right occasionally took comic forms. After the war when I had become a stockbroker he rang me at my office to say that Freddie de Guingand had told him he must buy some shares in a South African company called Consolidated Glass. "Is that the sort of thing you do?" he said. "Well, I want to buy £500 worth and you had better have some yourself. Freddie says they are the cat's whiskers." We bought the shares at eight shillings. After two years they were down to three shillings. The chimney of the factory had fallen down just before Monty went out to South Africa. While there he asked the Minister of Finance for a report on Consolidated Glass. The chairman, hearing that the Ministry of Finance was looking into his company because Monty had a few shares in it, wrote to Monty saying he would buy his shares back at eight shillings. Having heard the full story from Freddie I was understandably amused when Monty said at our next meeting: "Johnny, have you still got those Consolidated Glass shares?" When I replied that I had, he said airily: "Oh, I thought you knew about these things – I saw the red light and got out without loss."

Much has been written about Monty's relationship with Freddie de Guingand and how heartlessly he treated him towards the end of the war and thereafter. One knew in the desert not only how much he relied on his judgement but also that he enjoyed his company more than anyone else's. Evening after evening in the desert it was Freddie who would start up the light-hearted conversation in the mess from which Monty derived his vital relaxation. Time and time again Freddie repaired a relationship which Monty had strained to breaking point. The most notable example of this was Bedell Smith, Eisenhower's Chief of Staff, but there was a long list of others and I would go so far as to say that if it had not been for Freddie, Monty's relationship with others in the high command would have become impossible and he would have had to go. He burnt himself out for Monty and it hurt all of us that Monty could not bring himself to think more of his well-being in later years.

When the time came for me to go, I left him feeling that I had stayed the course, thanks to his acceptance of my youthful shortcomings. This he expressed to me in a letter of 10 October, 1946, as follows:

> 7, Westminster Gardens,
> Marsham Street, S.W.1
> 2-10-46

My dear Johnnie,

Thank you for your nice letter. I was very glad to have you with me on the trip to Canada and the U.S.A. We had stirring times together. If at times I was a bit difficult you will I am sure realize that I had a load to carry that can seldom have been given to anyone else: and the responsibility was immense. I value your friendship and, having been through so much together, we must not lose touch. Do come and see me here whenever you like; you can run in and out as you like; come and have a meal whenever you feel inclined.

> Yrs ever
> Montgomery of Alamein

How do you like civilian life?

He always had to be in command, but was tolerant of other people's attitude to life, whether he approved of it or not. He was considerate to each of us and often kind. When my son

Nicky was born, he said he would like to be godfather, so that "the boy can be brought up in the right way and not with some of your terrible habits". Nearly every birthday after he was six Nicky received a letter enclosing a £1 note with instructions that it should not be spent by his father. When he was fourteen I got a letter pointing out that Nicky was now to be led and not driven and I was to remember that. He would come to lunch with us regularly on the Sunday before Christmas. I always enjoyed my visits to the Mill and he certainly enjoyed telling one how hopeless all politicians were.

The loyalty which Monty seemed to command from so many who served under him, of all ranks from General to private, was extraordinary.* This was still evident when I set about the arrangements for his statue in Whitehall. This I could not have done without the help of John Harding and Denis Hamilton, but it was not only the response to the appeal for funds which astonished one but the innumerable letters received in his praise from serving soldiers and from widows or relations of those who had been killed while serving under him. When one came across a problem, which was bound to arise in trying to set a statue up in Whitehall, one only had to find someone in the Department involved who had served under him and the way was clear.

There was an inevitable sadness about the final years as his powers waned. The last time I went to see him, which can only have been a short time before he died, I had arrived after

---

* A sapper wrote home from Italy on 8 January, 1944, as follows:

"You will have heard by now that our leader, General Montgomery, has left us. I think I can say that everybody was extremely sorry to see him depart. He will be remembered by us not only for the battles he has won and has yet to win, but also for the perfect confidence and trust which we had in him and he in us. No one who has not been in the Eighth Army can appreciate just what he meant to us. He was more than a Commander or a General, he was a real human person. He never talked down to his men, but made them feel as though they were his equals. We hope he will win the confidence of his Army as well in his new assignment."

an hour and a half's drive. I went up to his bedroom and the first – and last – words he said were: "Johnny, I get very tired, you know. I think you had better go." It was good to see that authoritative command still there. I turned on my heel and left.

A Good Listener

Richard O'Brien

Sɪʀ RICHARD O'BRIEN ᴅꜱᴏ ᴍᴄ *(and bar) was born in 1920 and served with the Sherwood Foresters and the Leicester Regiment in North Africa, the Middle East, Italy and Greece. He was Personal Assistant to Montgomery 1945–1946. From 1958–1961 he was Director of Industrial Relations of the British Motor Corporation; from 1971–1976 Chairman of the CBI Employment Policy Committee; and from 1976–1982 Chairman of the Manpower Services Commission.*

I WALKED INTO the famous caravan one evening in the spring
of 1945. On the previous day I had arrived at Tactical Headquarters of 21st Army Group and was not in a happy frame of
mind. I had left my battalion in Southern Italy in response to
a command from Alexander, transmitted on behalf of the
Field-Marshal. He shook my hand, asked me to sit down and
began to give me a brief description of the battlefield in
North-West Europe as it stood at what were then the last few
weeks of the war. He did not ask me about myself and
assumed that I was pleased to be where I was. His sharp, nasal
delivery and curt style did not make a good impression on
me. It was not an auspicious beginning to my time at his
personal headquaters.

Weeks went by and after the end of hostilities we established ourselves in the schloss at Ostenwalde in Hanover
province. I was then a Liaison Officer and was billeted in a
house near the schloss. One evening I was invited to dinner –
the first such invitation I had received. It was, I remember, a
lively and stimulating occasion with Monty in cracking form.
He seemed to me to be a different person to the apparently
somewhat harsh individual I had met in the caravan – alert,
lively, curious and amusing. We talked about anything and
everything and especially the war in Italy from which I had
come. He led me in conversation in such a way that I found
myself giving vent to sweeping criticisms of the conduct of
the war in Italy seen from the point of view of an infantry
company commander. He enjoyed discussions of this kind

and was capable himself of very strong criticisms of his colleagues which he wouldn't hesitate to utter in front of young men like myself. Walking back across the courtyard I was appalled at my indiscretions and felt it likely that I should be summoned next morning to be rebuked. In fact, as I now realize, I could not have served my own ends better – he enjoyed nothing so much as lively critical discussions with the young on anything and everything except his own conduct of battles.

Later I moved into the schloss and lived with him for nine months or more as his Personal Assistant. It was an extraordinary time. We discussed anything and everything – except, I repeat, his own personal experiences. For example, I had views on the Battle of Alamein as seen from the point of view of a platoon commander in a motorized battalion supporting tanks. I could never get him to discuss this battle. No other matters were barred. We had the liveliest discussions on political and social questions, not least because I would put forward somewhat left-wing views which used to excite, amuse and stimulate him. His political views were much discussed at this time and there was even thought that he might enter politics. I am sure this was never his intention.

He was not a natural debater in public though fascinated by the play of ideas, including relatively radical ones in private. I would guess he voted Conservative, but he was not in any sense an establishment man. He distrusted the "old boy" network, privileged positions and all that was implied in them – and, especially, all forms of amateurism. Because he was a dedicated professional he had a deep distrust of those in the army who he believed had not taken their profession seriously, whether or not they were full-time or part-time soldiers. This accounted for the brusque treatment meted out to certain cavalry generals in the Desert, whose style and competence he distrusted in equal measure.

Our conversations ranged far and wide. It was a time when

he was throwing out and throwing off the preoccupations of battle. He wanted intellectual stimulus – and he seemed to thirst for information on social and political questions. Towards the Germans he had no prejudices and felt no hatred. His was the reaction of the fighting soldier to the enemy – respect for his professional qualities without, in his case, the obsessions about the Nazis which many of us felt. He would listen intently and sympathetically to my reports of the living conditions in the Ruhr and elsewhere. The post-war settlement of Europe was not much discussed, but my belief is that he had no doubt, even at that early stage, of Germany's place in it. Perhaps it was that he was more interested in the social and political issues in Britain than he was in grand political designs for Europe.

We also talked about the war and not least about the performance of fellow generals of whom (as I have said) he could be sharply critical. His thinking seemed to me to be dominated by his experience with both World Wars. He had fought in the trenches and was horrified by the loss of life. He was determined not to repeat the mistakes made by the First War generals. This may be the main explanation of the caution he showed in preparation for his battles. He wanted always to lose as few lives as possible – and he wanted also to ensure that the soldiers were properly looked after when they were not in the front line.

The marked separation of the commanding generals in Flanders from the troops under them made a great impression on him; he disliked the idea of living in relative luxury whilst the soldiers and the front-line officers were in the trenches. Both his natural caution and his interest in the soldiers' welfare led him to concentrate on logistics. He was concerned all the time with "the soldier's bootlaces"; he never forgot that he was commanding large numbers of individual soldiers who deserved to have their wants and needs attended to. Their morale was, he believed, crucial to success. It is no accident

that he published and widely circulated throughout the army
when CIGS a pamphlet entitled "Morale in Battle". It was
also no accident that in discussion with his then Adjutant,
Johnny Henderson, and myself, he agreed readily and immediately to devote his speech at Mansion House on 18 July,
1946, on receiving the Freedom of the City of London, to the
British Soldier and his qualities. He declared that the founda-
tions of the spirit of the British Army were to be found in the
independence, good humour and tolerance of the soldiers.
These three qualities produced the characteristic of endurance
in hardship, and the combination of good humour and tolerance bred comradeship. It was not so much the analysis but
the fact that he was willing to devote this historic occasion,
the first of its kind after his return to London, to the British
soldier that was significant.

My chief memory of him is his intense, lively and genuine
respect for what people were doing and thinking. This gave
him a willingness to listen and an openness of approach which
was highly stimulating. On a visit to him many years afterwards I recall that, after being introduced to my family,
he dismissed us all except my wife. He took her on one side
to discuss the social and education problems of the young
people (she is a child psychiatrist) she was then dealing with in
Birmingham. After some time with her he called me over and
we surveyed the current industrial scene, industrial relations,
attitudes of trade unions and so on. Later he gave time to my
children in whom also he would take a genuine interest. No
picture of him is complete without a recognition of this sharp,
sympathetic curiosity and interest in affairs generally and
especially in the thoughts and aspirations of the young. He
had liberated himself to a remarkable degree from the narrow
assumptions on which so many military men based their
opinions. This made him an attractive and stimulating person
to work with and for. People who do not know him may
be surprised by this; but it was so and it accounts for the

devotion and loyalty showed to him by those who worked closely with him.

I have only one other point to make. Monty seemed always able to convince himself that his decisions were right. He was extremely good at detecting the weak points in an argument or in a document, ruling them out of consideration and then making a decisive selection from a number of options. He could *choose* more incisively than anyone I have ever met – and having chosen could call the ideas out of the air and make them realities on the ground. With him, theory became action in no time; and because he showed conviction and generated confidence others would believe his decisions were right and would work energetically to carry them out. I certainly felt this – and so, I believe, did many others.

ADCs in North Africa – John Poston and Johnny Henderson

Bill Williams, Intelligence Officer, North Africa

Monty with HM King George VI and Johnny Henderson

The Liaison officers. The British officers (from left to right) are Tom Howarth, Peter Earle, John Poston, John Sharp, Dick Harden and Charles Sweeny; the US officers are Major Prisk and Major Frary

Education and Leadership

Tom Howarth

T. E. B. HOWARTH MC *was born in 1914 and served in the Hampshire Regiment and the King's Regiment. He was a liaison officer with Montgomery in 1945. He was successively Headmaster of King Edward's School Birmingham, Second Master of Winchester College, High Master of St Paul's School, Fellow and Senior Tutor of Magdalene College, Cambridge, and Headmaster of Campion School, Athens. He was a Trustee of the Imperial War Museum from 1964–1979.*

I was certainly the least professional soldier ever employed at Monty's small Tac Headquarters, about which so much has been written in this and other books. Having started as a private soldier in September, 1939, I had eventually graduated to a commission after distinctly "character forming" experiences in the sanitary squad and the quartermaster's store. By my sixth year of service I had more or less familiarized myself by dint of trial and error with what was required of me, but even so was totally astonished one day early in February, 1945, to be summoned from a cold and muddy battle which was going on in the Reichswald to report to Tac HQ as one of the Commander-in-Chief's small group of liaison officers. Initially I found some of my seven colleagues (two American) tough, desert-hardened young warriors like John Poston and Dick Harden rather more alarming than I did the Field-Marshal. After the first soul-stripping scrutiny which he imposed on anybody crossing his path, he was to treat me with consistent kindness and consideration for the next twenty-five years.

Like my colleagues I was despatched daily to various parts of the battlefield and would give an account of what I had seen and heard that evening to an audience in the caravan, which could on occasions include, as well as Monty, Churchill or Alanbrooke or Ismay. This was heady stuff for an obscure thirty-year-old, his head stuffed with Cambridge history, who suddenly – and totally improbably, as it seemed – was finding himself existentially involved in the historical process. Those caravan encounters were intensely educative. Under that penetrating gaze one learnt to say what one had to, neither more nor less, and never to waffle nor flannel; but if, as sometimes happened, one made a joke or turned a phrase which tickled his fancy he would give his high-pitched cry of laughter and repeat the remark so that he somehow appropriated it to himself. Quite quickly he imbued in me the confidence necessary to do the job more or less properly – he was *par excellence* a teacher – and I was greatly helped by increasingly frequent invitations to dine in his mess where, emboldened by the copious draughts of wine always available, I suppose I acquired something of the status of one of his licensed jesters.

Generally our daily missions served primarily to provide up-to-date battle intelligence and an early indication of the next day's battle plans. After saying our piece and marking up our section of the operations map, we usually knew little or nothing of what use would be made of our work. I recall an exception one evening when I reported much military confusion as a result of the US Ninth Army and General Dempsey's Second Army converging on one road. There and then Monty called up Dempsey and demanded in shrill tones, "Is that you, Bimbo? There seems to be a nonsense going on . . ."

But occasionally one was asked to do something rather different. He knew that I had served with the Third Division from Caen to the Reichswald and one day just before the end of the war he sent for me and said, "Tomorrow I want you to go to the Third Division and come back and tell me why they aren't fighting properly," a horrifying, and it could be argued totally improper, responsibility to impose on a very junior temporary major. But it is not of course the sort of information you can find out by exchanging letters.

By the end of the war, three of the eight LOs whom I had joined in February were casualties, John Poston and Charles

Sweeny dead and Peter Earle badly wounded. As a fortunate survivor, I stayed on at Tac, now the personal headquarters of a Military Governor rather than a Commander-in-Chief, until August, 1945, and thereafter worked briefly and incompetently in the Control Commission until demobilization in January, 1946. Of this period I have a few recollections which in different ways illuminate aspects of Monty's character. The first concerned the late General Sir John Sharp, who had recently joined the liaison team. John was at that time a spectacularly handsome young gunner officer decorated in the desert and as a regular evidently destined to a brilliant career in the Army.

Marshal Rokossovsky, commanding the Russian forces on our front, invited Monty and some of the staff to a party to celebrate the end of hostilities. To plan the meeting Monty sent over a divisional commander, who duly warned the Russians that Monty neither drank nor smoked, it being hoped that this would not be a cause of offence. One of the Russian officers after a moment's reflection commented, "My God, what must he do with women?", an observation greatly appreciated by Monty, who never tired of repeating it. At the reception a titanic quantity of vodka was on offer, much of which was directed at John, the youngest member of the party, who understandably enough felt called on to compensate for his commander's abstinence in the interest of allied good relations. The consequences were inevitable. Noel Chavasse, a notably quick witted ADC, just managed to spirit John into the aeroplane's lavatory and lock him in before the party ended. As it was breaking up Monty asked where John was and was told that he had gone ahead as he was feeling unwell. Everyone then boarded the plane while Monty stood on the steps and saluted the Russian guard of honour, who then proceeded to fire a salute of honour, answered shot for shot with his revolver by John Sharp through the lavatory window as a sort of *feu de joie*. During the three subsequent days which it took John to recover, the anger of the Chief (as we called him) loomed thunderously over Tac. He was predictably sent back to his unit, while the rest of us concluded that there, but for the grace of God, would we too have gone. We learnt shortly afterwards that Monty had carefully written to the CO of the unit to the effect that after an appropriate period of probation the young officer concerned should be encouraged to pursue his illustrious career.

My turn seemed to have come when I was ordered to join Kit Dawnay and Johnny Henderson in a trip to Paris in May, 1945, when Monty was to receive the Grand Cross of the Legion of Honour from de Gaulle in person. Almost at the last moment Monty decided that the occasion called for a public exposure of his schoolboy French in a speech he was scheduled to make at the end of his visit. In such circumstances anybody else would have carefully consulted some appropriate Foreign Office expert. Instead, I was sent for and told I must compose a short passage in French, which must extol the glories of French culture and mention by name not more than three of its most celebrated exponents. I concocted something reasonably appropriate about France as *la mère des armes, des arts et des lois* and nominated, more or less from the top of my head, Racine, Berlioz and Pasteur. We then had a pronunciation exercise. Shortly afterwards we set off in a Dakota accompanied by A. P. Herbert, dressed as a Petty Officer in the RNVR. I spent a good deal of the visit escorting A. P. H., who showed an enthusiasm I didn't share for going round and round the Place de la Concorde in a sort of rickshaw or human taxi which was the only form of available transport. However, I had an excellent view of the central ceremony itself during which de Gaulle, operating very literally *de haut en bas*, kissed Monty on both cheeks. The speech itself was delivered from the balcony of the British Embassy to a hero-worshipping crowd in the Rue St Honoré. The

English part went well and the cultural peroration, faithfully delivered in his Army Class accent, even better. Then suddenly to my horror he abandoned the text and, carried away by an onrush of idiomatic virtuosity, dismissed the whole parade with a peremptory: "Eh, maintenant allez-vous en!" The following Sunday's *Observer* carried an article commenting sagely on the extraordinary breadth of the Field-Marshal's interest in French culture.

Just before my short-lived period in the secretariat of the Control Commission, a vastly overstaffed organization which involved me at any rate in a degree of tedium, the like of which I have never encountered before or since, Monty had addressed a packed meeting of the Commission's officers. He asked me to find out how his lecture had gone. It had, in fact, been a total disaster and I had to tell him so. He was interested and took it very well, thereafter leaving them to get on with the job in their own particular way. I suspect this incident may have played a small part in discouraging him after the war from making mass speeches – an activity, of course, which greatly appealed to his vanity – unless specifically asked to.

In January, 1946, I returned to teaching at Winchester, where David Montgomery was briefly my pupil. I was to see a lot of Monty in the years ahead, primarily because of the intense interest which he took in schools. While this was largely centred on the public schools, it was not exclusively so – there is a Montgomery of Alamein school on the outskirts of Winchester, which was in those days a secondary modern. He was for several years a governor of The King's School, Canterbury, and of St Paul's. At the former he met more than his match in the redoubtable Canon Shirley whom he tried unavailingly for a long time to unseat as Headmaster. By dint of being made an honorary member of the Mercers' Company he also played a considerable role in the post-war history of his old school, St Paul's, characteristically telling me when I became High Master that "if you have any trouble with the other governors ring me up and I'll bring up the heavy artillery". He greatly enjoyed what he called "the headmaster stakes", lavishing advice freely to Governing Bodies on whom they should short list or "put in the paddock", as he would describe it.

But in many ways the apple of his eye was St John's, Leatherhead, a nineteenth century school originally founded for the sons of the clergy, of which he was a very active Chairman of the Governors from 1950 to 1966. In their centenary year, 1951, he persuaded Lord Rank to make over the proceeds of the film première of *The Lavender Hill Mob* and made a radio appeal himself; at his behest, an anonymous donor paid with a single cheque for the building of a new chapel; and on one occasion he entertained the entire cricket XI, unbeaten that year, for several days in his French château.

There were, I think, three particular reasons which accounted for his passion for schools and everything about them. First and foremost, he liked boys.* Perhaps in this post-Freudian era it should be said loud and clear that there is nothing wrong in that – it would not, after all, assist the advance of civilization if everybody disliked them, irritating as they usually are. Secondly, he had a considerable bee in his bonnet (and one which could buzz very tediously) about leadership. His view of the subject was overtly and unashamedly élitist and so ran counter to the whole ethos of post-war Britain. This did not, however, in the least deter him from darting about the country "spotting" potential leaders. Thirdly he was, of course, essentially didactic by temperament and liked a captive audience. Schools in his youth were not places where you argued – and he had no interest whatever in argument, unless conducted in jest.

* On this aspect of his character I find myself in entire agreement with Nigel Hamilton's careful analysis in *Monty, the Making of a General*, pp 22–23.

All these three strands combined to make him obsessively interested in head boys. He had at the back of his mind an ideal stereotype – the captain of the XV, straight-backed, short-haired, destined to win the sword of honour at Sandhurst. Readers of Mark Girouard's *The Return to Camelot* will recognize the type, frequently depicted by the illustrators of scouting manuals and *The Boys' Own Paper*. In short, somebody as far removed as possible from the "unhealthy" atmosphere of his maternal grandfather's *Eric or Little by Little*. I would be invited year after year to bring the school captain of St Paul's along to watch Monty present the trophies at the Royal Tournament at Olympia. Most years this was not altogether a success since my idea of what constituted a suitable school captain for a school like St Paul's tended to differ appreciably from his.

However, although he was always on the look out for what might be called "nature's head boys" he could be constructive and sympathetic with almost all aspects of youthful aspirations and difficulties. When I was Second Master at Winchester, and so in charge of the Scholars, he would often ask himself over for lunch in College Hall. He developed a great interest in the most formidable and argumentative small boy then in College, who is now a celebrated Friedmanite Professor of Economics. At a rather different level of sophistication, he sent me with evident satisfaction the following letter written on lined blue paper in an immature hand:

December the 30th 1967

Dear Field Marshall (sic) Montgomery,

I am the twelve-year old who accidentally bumped into you outside the Saville on the first night of "Iolanthe".

The incident was a small one for you no doubt, but for me it was a great one and, I will always look on it with great pride.

It was a great honour to have knocked into you and to have said a rather sheepish "Hello!" But in years to come I would need proof, so if you could find the time please would you answer this letter?

Please excuse the writing for it is my worst subject at school, apart from French, so when I become Field-Marshall I shall declare war on France (which is getting too big for it's (sic) boots) and when I have won I'll have the language abolished.

Yours sincerely,
Bruce M. Filliou

P.S. There is nothing really to answer in this letter so please could you sign your name on a piece of paper?

Monty did answer, – "I have asked him not to declare war on France when he becomes a Field-Marshal – adding that we are quite safe since he is unlikely to reach that rank. It is not too easy to become a Field-Marshal as I know well."

There were indeed a number of characteristics he shared with the young – impulsiveness and tactlessness in speech, an affection for budgerigars and other pets, the collector's instinct (in his case for freedom caskets and foreign decorations) and an uncritical enthusiasm for simple pleasures like *The Sound of Music* or the Royal Tournament. He liked small girls as well as small boys. When my very young daughter subjected him to a quite unsolicited kiss one day at Isington Mill he was vastly pleased and amused and wrote her the following letter when she was sixteen:

Isington Mill
17-3-66

My dear Frances,

I have been considering your visit here and have reached the conclusion that I would prefer you to come alone, and not to bring a friend. We can then have a good talk. I will be in London on Monday 18th April, as Parliament re-assembles that day and I will have to take the Oath of Allegiance to the Sovereign – which must always be done in a new Parliament. So I will call at the High Master's House in my car at about 5 p.m., and we will drive back here. On Tuesday 19th April, and on the 20th, I will take you shopping; and there is a very good ladies hair dressing saloon which you may like to attend!

The Queen opens Parliament, in State and wearing her Crown, on Thursday 21 April. I think you should attend that in the House of Lords. I will give you a ticket for the Long Gallery and the Queen will pass very near to you. You will have to be up at the House of Lords by 10 a.m. and you could not do that from here without a very early start. So I will send you back to your home by car on the evening of Wednesday 20th April.

The dress for yourself in the Long Gallery will be ordinary day dress, with hat.

All this will make a very good programme for you.

> Yrs. sincerely
> Montgomery of Alamein

In later years he greatly enjoyed indulging in self-parody. In 1970 a St Paul's boy called John Witt wrote asking if he and a school friend might pay him a visit. As a result I received the following:

> Isington Hill,
> Alton.
> 5/5/70

My dear Tom,

See enclosed from John Witt. Will you kindly inform him, and Philip W. (whoever he may be!) as follows:

1. I live 5 miles from Alton. My station is Bentley, which is one mile from my home.

2. Trains from Waterloo stop at Bentley only once every hour, at 11 minutes after the hour.

3. I cannot have them here in the morning. They must come in the afternoon.

4. They should catch the train which arrives Bentley at 3.11 p.m. It leaves Waterloo at 5 minutes to 2 p.m. They must ask at the barrier which is their part of the train, since it splits at Woking and if they get in the wrong part they will finish in Portsmouth.

5. On arrival Bentley Station they will walk to my house, asking the way frequently to Isington village. I am well known in these parts.

6. They can wear any old clothes they like. They must get their hair cut.

7. We can have a talk. I will give them tea, provided the hair has been cut.

8. Make certain Philip W. understands the problem.

Yrs. ever,
Montgomery of Alamein

His habit, again self-parodied, of repeating everything he said in a louder voice than the first time could have odd social consequences. He acquired the term "toilet" and would use it with a most un-Mitfordian relish on arrival in a new location. "What I need," he would say, "is the toilet – the *toilet*."

Bill Williams in Chapter Two has accurately described Monty's humour as banana-skin deep. Much of his clowning derived from his contempt for pomposity, so that the collapse of stout parties on banana skins afforded him intense pleasure. His favourite (and frequently repeated) anecdote related to a self-important personage who had been asked to address a high-level gathering of French officers and had rashly volunteered to speak in French. Fatally he began describing his own past life with the words: "*Quand je regarde mon derrière, je vois que c'est divisé en deux parties.*" Every time he told that story he would chortle with joy. "That's the way to put yourself in the *potage* – the *potage*" he would say. He also greatly enjoyed recalling a boyhood occasion when helping on the farm he had been instructed to take a cow's temperature and had mistaken the appropriate aperture. All good cleanish fun, as one might say.

He enjoyed the human comedy and never more so than towards the end of his life before his faculties were finally impaired, as he patrolled the garden at Isington Mill or expounded to visitors the background to his ostentatiously displayed trophies and mementoes. He could look back on a career in all respects extraordinary. Perhaps few things can have given him more satisfaction than a tribute which he received from an American source which serves to some extent to offset the chorus of transatlantic criticism. In a letter quoted on page 224 of the *Memoirs*, General Walter Bedell Smith, Eisenhower's Chief of Staff, wrote:

Dear General,

I have just received from a most reliable and intelligent source a report on attitude and state of mind of American troops in action. The writer is completely unbiased, and his report contains the following paragraph, which I hope will give you as much pleasure as it has given me:

"Confidence in the high command is absolutely without parallel. Literally dozens of embarking troops talked about General Montgomery with actual hero-worship in every inflection. And unanimously what appealed to them – beyond his friendliness, and genuineness, and lack of pomp – was the story (or, for all I know, the myth) that the General 'visited every one of us outfits going over and told us he was more anxious than any of us to get this thing over and get home.' This left a warm and indelible impression."

The above is an exact quotation. Having spent my life

with American soldiers, and knowing only too well their innate distrust of everything foreign, I can appreciate far better than you can what a triumph of leadership you accomplished in inspiring such feeling and confidence.

Faithfully

Bedell

The CIGS

Frank Longford

The EARL OF LONGFORD KG, PC *was born in 1905 and served at the outbreak of the war in the Oxfordshire and Buckinghamshire Light Infantry. Ill-health forced him to resign his commission and he later served with the Home Guard. He was Personal Assistant to Sir William Beveridge from 1941–1946, was appointed Parliamentary Under-Secretary of State at the War Office in 1946–1947 and thereafter held a long succession of ministerial and cabinet posts under successive Labour governments, being Leader of the House of Lords from 1964–1968. He is a publisher and philanthropist and the author of sixteen books.*

My memories of Lord Montgomery are vivid and cover a long period. In later years, especially after retirement, he frequently attended the House of Lords and I had tea with him there many times. In his heyday he probably filled the Chamber more rapidly than any non-official speaker. Nor did he confine himself to military matters. He made his maiden speech on the after-care of prisoners following an initiative taken by a young public relations officer called Peter Thompson supported by myself. I can still remember the phrase he applied to the Home Office arrangements at that time. "A dog's breakfast," he called them. He must be given some credit at least for subsequent improvements.

He always enjoyed meeting young people, Peers or Commoners. One day I was giving lunch to Philip Moore, my Private Secretary at the Admiralty, now Principal Private Secretary to the Queen. As Monty passed our table I introduced Philip Moore to him. "Philip," I said, "played rugger for England." Monty was on the alert at once. "Rugger," he said, "I used to be keen on rugger. I was quite good at rugger." (He captained St Paul's.) "But now I am more involved in soccer. I am more involved in soccer. Last Saturday I was at Wembley. I was introduced to a young man called Wright. I was told that he was the Captain of England. I said to him, 'I was Captain of England myself at one time.' Wright asked me, 'When were you Captain of England, sir?' I replied, 'In the war. In the war.'" I hope that the very extravagance of this claim will convince old friends of the Field-Marshal that the story is authentic.

It was during these last years that I went to stay with him at the Mill which I deemed a signal honour. I had been told that by that time he was lonely, but he was not only a generous but an exuberant host. We shared a common desire to see Germany re-arm as quickly as possible and brought back into Western partnership. His influence in that direction was, of course, vastly greater than mine. But I think that it pleased him that I who had been Minister for Germany and earlier taught International History at Oxford should see matters in the same way as he did.

In 1953 Doctor Adenauer, the German Chancellor, paid an official visit. Monty and I were standing together after a dinner at No 10 Downing Street, our host being Sir Winston Churchill. Churchill at one point lumbered round among his guests exuding benevolence. Monty rather enjoyed in his dealings with me the role of a tough soldier teasing an absent-minded intellectual. He noticed that my hair, though absent from the dome of my head was very fluffy at the sides. "Don't you think he wants his hair cutting?" he asked Sir Winston. Churchill paused and then replied very deliberately. "Your head – my dear Field-Marshal – requires compression – under a military cap. He needs his – for speaking – in the House of Lords." Monty gave a good show of enjoying the joke.

But as sometimes happens he made the sharpest impression when I got to know him first. That is to say when I became Under-Secretary for War in Autumn, 1946. Monty, CIGS, was still very much a national hero. My secretary, a middle-aged lady, used to ask me to excuse her if she heard the Field-Marshal was leaving the building for lunch. A small crowd was always waiting to cheer him on his way. I myself had begun the war as a private in the infantry and finished as a private in the Home Guard. It may sound strange today but I had actually persuaded Attlee to allow me to serve in the War Office rather than one of the social departments which he first offered me. If I could not do anything in the Army I could at least do something for the Army. Never did Monty so much as hint that my war record was less than glorious.

On my first day in the War Office Oliver Baldwin, the gifted but eccentric son of the former Prime Minister, gave a drinks party for me to meet the Generals. "What I like about the New US of S (Under-Secretary of State)," said Oliver, "is that he doesn't pretend to have had a good war. Now you fellows, you're all covered with medals but which of you saw active service in the front line in the Second World War?" Answer came "None". One of the Generals eventually summoned the courage to ask Oliver, "Where did you see active service in the Second World War, Oliver?" "Eritrea," he replied conclusively.

Monty, however, was not present. He didn't drink and in any case he was rather too grand. I enquired whether I was supposed to go to see him or should I ask him to come to see me? I was his theoretical superior and on one or two occasions presided over the Army Council in the absence of the Secretary of State. I was told that, strictly speaking, I could request him to come to see me but that it was more tactful to go to see him unless he took the initiative for some reason of his own.

I remember going to dinner with him and enjoying it immensely, but I recall just as clearly his account of giving dinner at his flat to Aneurin Bevan. Bevan was regarded as the main anti-militarist in the Cabinet. I helped to arrange this visit to Monty for dinner. I asked the latter next day how it had gone. Monty was very pleased with the event. I asked him what they had talked about. Did they argue at all about controversial matters? Monty replied complacently, "I asked him entirely about his family. He spent the whole evening telling me about his family. I understand him perfectly now.

An excellent evening." I never managed to elicit from Nye Bevan how he felt it had gone.

Monty took me down to the Staff College at Camberley on one memorable occasion. There were in my recollection, possibly inflated, several hundred officers in uniform. I, the only civilian present, perched uneasily on the platform while Monty delivered a spellbinding address. He ended this way: "And remember, gentlemen. Never forget, gentlemen, the politicians." All eyes turned in my direction. "They are our masters (considerable laughter). It's up to us – to lead them – up the garden path – (the laughter now was happy and pro-longed) gentlemen dismiss."

Perhaps the most flavoured of his interventions in the House of Lords arose during the Committee stage of Lord Arran's Private Members' Bill to legalize homosexual be-haviour in private between consenting adults. A Bill of this kind was passed into law two years later. It was proposed in the Bill that an adult should be deemed to be a person over twenty-one. There were some who thought that at eighteen one was old enough to make up one's own mind on sexual matters. Others thought contrariwise that the age limit should be raised to twenty-five. Monty "brought the House down" by handing in a manuscript amendment (he was up to all the devices) which laid it down that the right age was eighty. His reasons must be given in his own language: "The purpose of that, of course, is that after the age of eighty it does not really matter what we do. I myself am rising 78, and the great thing is that at the age of eighty at least one has the old age pension to pay for any blackmail which may come along." Loud laughter. Lord Stonham for the Government later commented, "I appreciate that this amendment is put forward, at least I hope it is, with the idea of good clean fun and anything that is good clean fun on a subject such as we are discussing is most welcome."

Monty, however, did not leave the matter there. "I regard

the act of homosexuality," he went on, "in any form, as the most abominable bestiality that any human being can take part in and which reduces him almost to the status of an animal. The time will come when we shall have to choose a title for this Bill, and I think that instead of 'Sexual Offences Bill (HL)' the proper title should be 'A Charter for Buggery' " (More laughter but some signs of dissent as the seriousness became more evident).

We often had tea together. On this occasion I asked him why he had not pressed his amendment to a division. He looked at me knowingly. "You must read – what I have written – about limited objectives. You must read – what I have written – about limited objectives." What, I asked him, was your limited objective this time? He replied without hesitation, "To make a nonsense of the whole thing. To make a nonsense of the whole thing." It was beyond the power of any one man to turn back the tide of homosexual law reform but no one could have tried harder than Monty.

One other anecdote among many which swim back into my mind. I had been to dinner with him at a time when there was a good deal of labour unrest and criticism among Conservatives of the British working man. "Your British working man," said Monty, "is all right. 80 per cent of British working men are good chaps. I could lead them anywhere. 15 per cent are neutrals neither one thing nor the other. I could lead them anywhere, anyone could lead them anywhere. 5 per cent are stinkers. You go and tell Clem Attlee and Ernie Bevin that all they've got to do is to have a showdown with the stinkers. A first-class row. Then they'll be in power for a thousand years." For some time afterwards when I ran into him he used to ask me, "How's that showdown with the stinkers? What's happened to the row?"

It is not within my competence to pass a verdict on Monty as a general, or even as a force in politics, but at a time when I was a nervous young Minister and when he could have made things extremely awkward for me, he did precisely the opposite. He strengthened my morale with as sure a touch as that which he exhibited at the head of great armies. I shall always fervently echo the words which, in my recollection, were used about him by Professor Michael Howard: "Nothing can ever diminish the gratitude which we owe him for his services to the nation or the respect which we feel for him as a man."

A Family Friend

Mary Soames

LADY SOAMES DBE, *the youngest daughter of Sir Winston and Lady Churchill's five children, was born in 1922. During the war she served in the ATS (now WRAC) in mixed anti-aircraft batteries in the UK and NW Europe. In 1947 she married Captain Christopher Soames (now Lord Soames); they have five children.*

Mary Soames' biography of her mother, Clementine Churchill, published in 1979, won a Wolfson Prize for History, and the Yorkshire Post Prize for Best First Work in 1979.

"He really is a thrilling and interesting personage – naive and sincere, good-tempered, and with the same sort of conceit which we read Nelson had. He has piercing blue eyes and a wirey young figure." Thus wrote Clementine Churchill on 3 January, 1944, in one of her long "round-robin" letters from Marrakesh to her family at home. Winston Churchill had fallen gravely ill with fatigue and pneumonia in early December, 1943, on his way back to England from the Teheran Conference. Arrived at Carthage to see General Eisenhower, he, at last, had admitted he could go no further. Kind 'Ike' placed his house there at Churchill's entire disposal, and there he, and Sarah (his daughter, an officer in the WAAF, acting as his ADC) and his immediate staff quickly reinforced by nurses and specialists, remained for nearly a month. Clementine Churchill flew out shortly afterwards to be with him. By the New Year Winston was enough recovered to move on to Marrakesh in Morocco to convalesce. He had very soon gathered up the reins of the war again, and both in Carthage and now in Marrakesh, a stream of service chiefs and political advisers flowed through the house.

As Winston grew stronger picnics became a feature of the daily programme. On New Year's Day, 1944, the party, including General Sir Bernard Montgomery, who was at that time commanding 21st Army Group, had picnicked by the foothills of the Grand Atlas. Clementine Churchill had probably met General Montgomery before, but this was the first time she had, so to speak, "taken him in". On the way to their picnic destination the General had driven with Winston, but on the homeward journey he went in Clementine's car. She noted that he was "frightfully pleased because, going slowly round some curves he was reconized by an old Frenchman with whom he had a long conversation". The General could not dally: "After dinner he flew home," Clementine continued in her letter, "and Sarah who for security reasons has been in mufti since her arrival here, put on her new Austin Reed uniform (22 coupons – not yet raised) to see him off." During this visit their conversation had evidently ranged over events and conditions on the "home front", including mixed anti-aircraft batteries, in one of which her youngest daughter, myself, was serving. On these subjects Clementine had found Sir Bernard woefully (if excusably) ignorant: he had after all been occupied in foreign parts with our armies! But Clementine ended her description of his visit with the amused comment: "This poor ignorant General did not know about mixed batteries or in fact about anything that goes on in England. I hope he will pick all this up soon!"

This brief encounter in North Africa was to be the prelude to a long and increasingly warm and close friendship between Winston and Clementine and their family and the great, and to us, lovable, Monty. With Winston, of course, he had a professional relationship, accounts of which can be found elsewhere; but there grew up between the two men an "out of school" friendship, which was to endure. But I think Monty was at once drawn to Clementine; this was not strange, for she had great warmth and charm, and she had taken at once to this most unusual man.

During their conversations in Marrakesh, it had emerged that one of Monty's great friends was Dr Hewlett Johnson, the Dean of Canterbury, widely known as the "Red Dean" for his pro-Soviet sympathies. Much of Clementine's time was taken up at this period with her work for the Appeal for the Red Cross Aid to Russia Fund, of which she was Chairman. Started in 1941, the Appeal had raised an enormous amount of money, and soon it became known as Mrs Churchill's Fund. There were other funds for sending help to Russia, but all of them had a political bias, and none of them had caught the imagination of the public to the extent of the Red Cross Appeal headed by Clementine. However, the largest of the "competitors" in that field was the Joint Aid Committee (Joint Committee for Soviet Aid) under the leadership of the Red Dean. Inevitably there was from time to time a spirit of competitiveness between the rival funds, and particularly between the one headed by Mrs Churchill and that sponsored by Dr Hewlett Johnson. Clementine had never actually met the Red Dean, but had frequently been irritated by his pro-Communist pronouncements. Monty suggested that he should arrange a meeting between them, to which Clementine readily agreed. During the spring of 1944, Monty therefore invited them both to lunch with him at the Army and Navy Club. It all passed off most amicably, although Monty later told me that my mother was coiled and ready to spring into battle! Indeed, their meeting led to an agreeable exchange of letters between Clementine and the Red Dean, followed up by her sending him as a present a picture which the Dean had admired at an exhibition and wished to buy, but found it had already been snapped up by Clementine.

Monty fully understood, and no doubt respected, Winston's deeply felt desire to "see things for himself", and his predilection for getting as close to the action as possible. He therefore welcomed him very soon after D-Day to make a tour of the battlefront in Normandy. Later, in March, 1945, shortly after British troops had crossed the Rhine, Winston made a two-day visit to the Field-Marshal's Headquaters. Clementine at that moment was on her way to Moscow for a six-week visit at the invitation of the Russian Red Cross.

During a break in her journey in Cairo on 28 March, she wrote to Monty:

> My dear Sir Bernard,
> I am perched here for 24 hours on my way to Moscow.
> I want to send you my heartfelt and grateful congratulations and rejoicings upon the Forcing of the Rhine – a glorious Victory which will for ever live in history when we have departed from this earthly scene. . . .

She had already heard from Winston about his visit to the battle front, and she went on:

> Winston loved his visit to you. He said he felt quite a reformed character and that if in earlier days he had been about with you I should have had a much easier life! Referring I suppose to his chronic unpunctuality and to his habit of changing his mind (in little things) every minute! . . .

Monty replied:

> Dear Mrs Churchill,
> Thank you so very much for your letter written from Cairo; it was kind of you to write as you did.
> It was a great pleasure to have the P.M. at my H.Q. during the Battle of the Rhine; he was very amenable to discipline and never argued about what was to be done! . . .

Very soon members of our family began to appreciate how kind and thoughtful Monty could be. In early 1945 the mixed heavy anti-aircraft battery with which I was serving as an ATS officer was posted to Belgium to form part of the defences of Brussels and then Antwerp, which were both still under the threat of bombardment by flying bombs or V-2 rockets. My battery was deployed on a (at first snow-covered and subsequently muddy) hilltop about fifteen miles from Brussels; the conditions were fairly spartan. I wrote my mother long letters about my life "on active service", but, of course gave no indication to her of our exact location, and the official postal address of my unit was merely a jumble of letters and numbers. My mother, used to knowing secrets of a more vital order, was somewhat frustrated by this minor mystery. However, she was presently informed of my actual and exact whereabouts by none other than the Commander-in-Chief himself! On 17 February, 1945, she wrote with a distinct note of triumph:

> I know exactly where you are. Who do you think told me? Your "Boss" [Field-Marshal Montgomery] who sent Captain Chavasse to look you up. He says "I sent an ADC (Noel Chavasse) to visit Mary and to ensure that all was well.
>
> Her battery is at . . . about 10 miles south-west of . . ., and they all seem to be well housed and to be enjoying themselves; morale generally is very high, so that seems very satisfactory.
>
> I have not had time to visit her myself; just at the present I am very occupied: on German soil I am glad to say!!"

Naturally great had been my own and my comrades' surprise and delight when, one day, quite unannounced, a jeep with very grand markings had driven up to our hilltop, out of which got the gallant Captain Chavasse MC, bearing chocolates and cigarettes for us all, and full of kind enquiries from his Chief. Both my own and Monty's stock took a steep rise!

Later that same year after the (for us) débâcle of the General Election in July, I again experienced kindness from Monty. By this time my battery had moved to Germany, where we were with several other units encamped on a large airfield not far from the flattened city of Hamburg. With the ending of hostilities our role had changed, and we were guarding and tending equipment of all description which was being handed in by various regiments; the airfield was a vast gun and vehicle park. In early August we were visited by the Field-Marshal. I was one among a group of officers standing near the small aircraft waiting for the great commander's departure. Someone must have told him I was there, for just before he climbed into his 'plane he came over to talk to me. In a letter to my mother I wrote:

> He was charming and kind and wanted to know how Papa was, and he asked specially about you. He really was kind and said that should you need me it could be arranged for me to be flown back. So I thanked him and said I would remember what he said in case of need.

In fact about a month later I was given a home posting at my request, through "the usual channels", but I shall always remember Monty's sensitivity and thoughtfulness at that time.

For the first few years of the hard-won peace, there does not seem to have been much contact between Winston and Clementine and Monty. There was no diminution of regard on either side, but Monty was Chief of the Imperial General Staff, and in addition to the pressure of the job it may well be that a too-close relationship with Winston Churchill, then Leader of the Opposition, who was battering the Government on every possible occasion, might have been awkward. But after he ceased to be CIGS in 1948 and his subsequent appointments were of a European nature, there is not a year between 1949 and 1964 (the last year Winston and Clementine lived at Chartwell) when "Montgomery of Alamein" and later, more relaxedly, "Montgomery of A" does not appear at least once or twice and, as the years went by, an increasing number of times in the Chartwell Visitors' Book. He seems to have come mostly for day visits in the earlier years, and then took to staying a day or two. When Winston was once again Prime Minister, from 1951 to 1955, Monty was also a guest at Chequers, both on official and personal grounds. Between 1948 and 1958 he was based in France, first as Chairman of the European Commanders-in-Chief Committee, and subsequently from 1951 to 1958 when he was Deputy Supreme Allied Commander in Europe, but he never let this affect his keeping-up with his friends.

After my marriage in 1947 to Christopher Soames we came to live at Chartwell, in the farmhouse at the bottom of the hill, and Christopher took on the management of my father's farm. There was a great deal of to-ing and fro-ing between the big and little houses, and so Christopher and I, and our rapidly increasing brood, were nearly always "on parade" for Monty's visits. After lunching at Chartwell, if it were springtime/summertime, there would often be a game of croquet. Monty played very well, but was closely matched by my mother, whom he loved to out-manoeuvre. Other guests, children and the senior grandchildren made up the croquet parties. Winston was a spectator, watching with keen interest the strategy and tactics of the game, and often providing pointful comments and suggestions. Very often after this my parents would bring Monty down to our farmhouse for nursery tea. No one could have been more genial, cosy and kind than Monty on these occasions. Soon we all got by heart a verse he would never fail to recite:

> Pudding time comes every day
> When the meat is cleared away.
> We all turn round and look to see
> What the pudding's going to be.

> We clap our hands if up there comes
> A lovely pudding stuffed with plums:
> But wholesome things like treacle rice
> We do not find so very nice.

(I gather from David Montgomery that this poem was also a feature of HIS nursery days!)

Such was our affection as well as regard for Monty, that when our third child and second son was born in May, 1952, we asked him to be a godfather. He accepted to do so, and no child could have had a more attentive and kindly concerned godparent. Jeremy Bernard Soames was christened that summer in St Mary's, Westerham; the church was full of friends and relations, and crowds outside greeted the two great men, Winston Churchill and Field-Marshal Montgomery. Afterwards, at a sunshine tea party in our garden, Monty raised his glass with us all as my father proposed the toast to "Christ's new faithful soldier and servant".

On several of his visits to Chartwell Monty brought his son David, then in his early twenties; on other occasions he would bring one of his other godsons, including Nigel Hamilton, who one day was to write with such brilliance his great godfather's life. In March, 1953, when Winston was again Prime Minister, and Coronation preparations were in full swing, Monty asked Clementine if he could bring his Page, Nicholas Wright, aged nine (up in London from school to try on his Coronation outfit) to tea at No 10. Our children were there to see their famous friend, and, of course, Jeremy, his godson, was particularly in evidence, although only just over a year old. Monty had given some firm instructions in his letter to my mother: "It is essential that Winston should look in at the tea party, if only for five minutes. Will you issue the necessary orders?" I cannot now recall if my father did "parade": but I'm sure he would have tried to do so, both on account of his partiality for Monty and "nursery tea" with his grandchildren.

The Château de Courances

A friend of the family. Monty and Lady Churchill

Christmas Day 1950. Monty at Pluckley with his son David, Tom Reynolds and Mrs Reynolds

"Le Petit" Marechal from the big Field-Marshal of England Montgomery of Alamein F.M.

Monty's little Swiss friend

Monty in Dublin for Alan Howarth's wedding, in the background De Valera

The friendship between Monty and Winston and Clementine was now firmly sealed, and he had become a regular and much enjoyed feature of our family's life. I know he enjoyed and set store by his relationship with both my parents, finding particularly with my mother a warmth and easy affection which may have helped to fill a void in the life of this unusual and patently lonely man, whose whole existence was in male and military circles, and who, because of his eminence and fame, found himself nearly always surrounded by those inferior in rank to himself.

The earlier letters "Dear Mrs Churchill . . . Yours ever, Montgomery of Alamein" by 1953 had progressed to being signed "Monty". Soon it was "My dear Clemmie . . . Yrs ever [or always] Monty". Clementine, too, thawed out on paper about the same time with "My dear Monty", but for quite a little time still signing herself "Clementine S. Churchill". It is not until the later 'fifties that we find letters "My dear Monty . . . Yours very affect: Clemmie". But her genuine liking and affection were ahead of her epistolary formulas. While her friendship helped to assuage some of the aridity of his personal life, Clementine would from time to time give him a good "ticking off", not allowing any "Montyish" lapses to pass. He always took her reprimands – which could be quite fierce – in good part, for not only was he fond of her, but I think he respected the "steel" in her character, and the high personal integrity and public standards she had always set herself as well as others.

It is always easy to make fun of the foibles or failings of great men. It was impossible not to be gently amused by dear Monty's "photograph" mania. Every one of his godchildren and many of his friends must certainly possess an album full of photographs (meticulously signed, dated, and often annotated) ranging from studio portraits to "candid" snaps. Perhaps he did overdo this a bit. All the same I'm sure (and indeed I hope) our Jeremy's grandchildren will look with interest (and some reverence) at the book of the Field-Marshal's Orders of the Day to his troops, inscribed and signed for his godson.

The great commander could also be quite authoritarian outside the limits of his vast parade ground. I find a letter from the earlier days of their friendship; after thanking my mother for a visit to Chartwell in August, 1952 he goes on to admonish:

> Winston's health is vital to the British people.
> There is much still to be done and the next two years are enormously important: not only in purely British affairs but also in my line of European security.
> He must keep well and happy.
> We need him at the helm for two more years.
> Tell him this from me.
>
> Yrs ever
> Monty

I do not know whether my father saw this letter. He might possibly not have appreciated his tenure of office being prescribed for him by a Field-Marshal, however eminent! In the event he overstayed Monty's ration by eight months.

But many more of Monty's letters were charmingly natural and appreciative, and sometimes very touching. After a visit to Chequers in September, 1953, he wrote to Clementine from his Headquarters at the Château de Courances: "I always enjoy my visits to you and Winston enormously; they are a delightful break in my life, and we have such great fun and laughter. May you both live to a ripe old age, and enjoy the best of health and happiness."

And after lunching with Winston and Clementine to celebrate his sixty-sixth birthday later that year he wrote this letter:

Isington Mill,
Alton,
Hants.
17 Nov., 1953

My dear Clemmie,

Thank you so very much for the delightful birthday lunch party you gave me: cake and all. It was really kind of you. On such occasions as my birthday, one feels rather lonely: with David away in Malaya and being all alone here. Kindness such as yours makes a very great difference. Thank you my very dear Clemmie.

Yrs always
Monty

The years 1953 and 1954 saw both Winston and Monty struck by ill health. In June, 1953, at the height of the festivities surrounding the Coronation, Winston sustained a stroke, which, starting mildly, intensified in its effects over a period of days. He had left No 10 while still able to walk, and so the real nature and extent of his illness remained for many months a well-kept secret. Among the relatively small number of friends who were admitted in those anxious days to Chartwell was Monty. The following year he himself had to have a severe operation. It was at the end of May, 1954, and my mother was away in Aix-les-Bains, trying to rid herself of the painful and exhausting neuritis from which she suffered a great deal at this time. I was at Frinton holidaying with my children, but I had instructions from my mother to keep closely in touch with Monty's progress. The Matron of the hospital treated me almost as "family", and so I was able to write pretty accurate news to my mother. Both the invalids, as we know, made remarkable recoveries, and indeed lived to fight many more days.

Monty fully appreciated what Winston's final resignation as Prime Minister would mean to him. He was invited to the party at No 10 attended by the Queen and the Duke of Edinburgh on the eve of Winston's resignation, as were many friends and comrades from many parts of his life. In writing to Clementine to say he would fly over from France in order to attend this occasion, Monty said, "We must all rally round him [WSC] in the next months and help him over some difficult days. I hope I may be allowed to look in on you from time to time, to play my part . . ." He did indeed, and over the years that remained Monty was to be as faithful and assiduous a friend as ever he had been in the days of action and glory.

Once Winston had retired from public office, Clementine took the opportunity to go abroad from time to time for brief holidays. Her own health had been far from good, and the strain and effort of Winston's last period as Prime Minister was taking its toll. Monty would often arrange to visit Winston during her absences, knowing how much he would be missing her; after each visit he would report to Clementine. One such letter written when Clementine was in St Moritz runs:

Trianon Palace Hotel,
Versailles,
Seine-et-Oise,
France
7 August 1955

My dearest Clemmie,

I spent the day at Chartwell yesterday and had lunch with Winston. We spent the afternoon at the bathing pool with Mary and her children; they are delightful and my Godson is just perfect.

Dear Winston. He is missing you I think but would not say so. In his old age he is so gentle, and courteous, and considerate. I think it does him good to go and see him, and tell him what is going on in my particular sphere in the international world in which I move. I would do anything for him . . ."

The following year Winston and Clementine invited Monty to spend Christmas with them at Chartwell; he was touched and grateful, but wrote to say he had already asked some old friends to be with him at Isington Mill; but he came for a New Year visit. After 1961, when Winston and Clementine ceased to be at Chartwell in the winter months, Monty spent one or two Christmas-times with them at 28 Hyde Park Gate in London.

Winston was inordinately fond of animals and birds, and during these years he had, as well as a chocolate poodle and a beautiful marmalade cat, a charming and most companionable blue budgerigar called "Toby". This little bird became quite famous and travelled about with him everywhere. He used to fly loose in his bedroom, nibbling the top of any book Winston was reading. At meals Toby would wend his way among the glasses and salt cellars, and was generally a great distraction. Monty had admired Toby, and so Winston procured a similar bird as a present for him. I don't know if it ever became as tame as Toby, but in one of his letters to Clementime, Monty reported that: "The budgerigar given to me by Winston is well and my corporal is teaching it to talk; I only hope it will not be taught unsuitable words."

In February, 1958, Winston was staying, as he often did in these latter years, with Emery and Wendy Reves at their beautiful villa, La Pausa, at Roquebrune. Clementine had not gone out there with him, but planned to join him later on. In mid-February Winston developed a chest cold, which quickly became pneumonia. Fortunately at this moment Clementine arrived, because this was the onset of a quite serious illness which lasted over many weeks. During this time Monty came to La Pausa for a few days, and his visit was most opportune and a great comfort to Clementine, who was worried by Winston's illness and wished very much they were at home. She afterwards wrote to me that "his [Monty's] visit has been a great tonic". In the same letter she told me that they had been for a walk one day in Menton and had gone "into a beautiful old church and burnt 2 candles for Papa". After Monty's return to his Headquarters at Versailles, he kept closely in touch. In a letter dated 19 March, starting "My very dear Clemmie", he tells her he has rung Christopher and me up to put us in the picture, and goes on: "I did so enjoy being with you both, and particularly our walks together – just ourselves alone, without any others. I shall telephone daily and keep in touch with Winston's progress, and with your plans. My love to you both. Yrs ever Monty."

Winston took quite a little while to recover from this illness, which in retrospect one realizes saw the beginning of a marked decline in his health and strength; it was from then on that he had a full-time nurse. Later that year Winston and Clementine celebrated their Golden Wedding on 12 September; they were staying with Max Beaverbrook at his villa, La Capponcina. Letters, telegrams, flowers and presents flooded in and quite one of the most touching letters was from their old friend Monty:

> This brings you my love and best wishes for the 12th September – to you both. I do not send you a present in gold. There is nothing I can give you which you have not already got – nothing tangible, that is.
> But I do give you both my deep and abiding affection and admiration – more a spiritual than a tangible gift, and possibly more lasting.

Clementine was a careful reader of the newspapers, and in October, 1956, after Monty had made an important speech

on defence and international implications, Clementine had
written to him approvingly:

October the 14th '56
28 Hyde Park Gate
London S.W.7

My dear Monty,

This is just a line of warm congratulations on your
speech. It was splendid.

I see the Russians are a bit cross; but we can't help that,
and they will get over it.

Your very affect:
Clemmie

But, great friend though he was, Monty did not always
bask in the sunshine of our smiles. There was the GREAT
COMMON MARKET RUMPUS! In July, 1962, Winston
was staying in the Hotel de Paris at Monte Carlo when he fell
and broke his hip. He was flown back to London and oper-
ated on. Subsequently he had to remain in the Middlesex
Hospital for nearly six weeks, during which time the world
press encamped outside the hospital, eager for news of the
patient, and also monitoring his visitors, among whom was
Monty. Just at this time, within months of the French veto of
the United Kingdom's entry to the European Community,
there was continuing discussion and party political controversy
about the whole question of British relationship with Europe.
On emerging from the hospital on 14 August, Monty was
surrounded by reporters who wanted to know how his friend
was progressing, and one of them asked him what they had
talked about. Monty then proceeded to say that in discussing
current affairs, Winston had expressed himself strongly against
this country joining the Common Market. This remark
was eagerly seized upon and widely published, and used as
a weapon by those newspapers who were in opposition to

the Government's intention to apply for membership. It was particularly embarassing also because the Commonwealth Prime Ministers' Conference was due to take place in mid-September.

Winston was much put out by his friend's mischievous indiscretion, and through his Private Secretary, Anthony Montague-Browne, he issued a statement to the Press which quoted from a letter he had sent to his Constituency Chairman almost exactly a year before this incident. In his last years as a Member of Parliament Winston attended the House regularly when he was not abroad, and although now he did not take an active part he was always at pains to keep his constituency party informed of his views on crucial issues, by writing letters to his Constituency Chairman which were released to the Press. In the letter dealing with his views on whether Britain should join the European Community Winston had maintained a neutral position, but had stated that the Government should certainly apply for membership in an exploratory fashion. In the statement given out in this summer of 1962, it was stated that his views had not changed. After 1955 when Winston had ceased to be Prime Minister, and during the Premierships of Anthony Eden and Harold Macmillan, he had always been at pains to give his support to them. Monty's gratuitous gaffe therefore in reporting part of a private conversation (at a time when, in any case due to his illness Winston had not been following public affairs with great assiduity) was a great embarrassment to him. Winston may have been annoyed and embarrassed – his family was outraged!

When all this broke in the newspapers, Christopher (who was then Minister of Agriculture and in Harold Macmillan's Cabinet) and I, with our children, were all in the north of Scotland. On 21 August, in a long letter to my mother about all our daily doings, I wrote:

"I have just written a letter to Monty reproaching him in round terms for his contemptible behaviour in repeating what Papa said to him in private. Are you furious? And have you had words with him or not? You know I love him, but I am outraged by his caddishness. So I wrote and told him . . . Do put me in the picture." My mother replied two days later: "I'm glad you wrote to Monty. I just couldn't. The whole sad incident made me quite sick." She then went on to tell me about the statement my father had issued, adding: "Not a word from Monty – He has had a very bad press . . ."

But Monty did write – and very handsomely too. A few days later my mother sent me a copy of the letters exchanged.

24 August 1962

My very dear Winston,

Now that you are back home I write to say how very very sorry I am about my indiscretions to the Press about our conversation in your hospital bedroom. I had myself just left hospital after three weeks in bed and maybe was not quite myself; such a thing has never happened before.

But whatever the circumstances it was completely unpardonable on my part and I am most deeply distressed to have involved you in a public controversy.

I hope it does not mean that you will never speak to me again. My affection and regard for you, and for Clemmie also, is beyond my power to express adequately; but you would both have every right if you decided that was to be my punishment.

Can you ever forgive me?

Yours always
Monty

25 August 1962

My dear Monty,

Thank you so much for your letter which puts every-thing right. Of course I forgive you, dear Monty.

We hope we may see you a little later on.

Yours ever,

W

As for my outburst – although Monty noted that he had received "an impertinent letter from Mary Soames" (which I'm afraid was true) – he wrote me this letter from Isington on 24 August:

My dear Mary,

I have your reprimand. It is very well deserved. I never thought for one moment it would create such a furore . . . The feeling that I have upset you all is most distressing, the more so since I have such a deep affection for Winston and Clemmie – and for you and your family. I hope it does not mean you will never speak to me again; you would have every right if you decided that was to be my punishment. I write in great distress.

Yrs ever

Monty

Well, of course we all kissed and made up, and all was forgotten and forgiven, and the true tenor of the genuine friendship between us all was soon resumed.

But now, since his accident in that summer of 1962, Winston's health and form generally declined even further. These last two and a half years of existence which were left to him were a sad, slow twilight. But he was ever surrounded by love and devotion, and from many thousands of people, veneration, which filtered through the advancing shades. Monty was ever the faithful friend in these latter days.

Clementine's health was at times as great a cause for anxiety as Winston's; the burden of the years was oppressing her now, and in 1963, particularly, she had several months of illness and retreat. Monty was much concerned and kept in close touch with me also. He would come to Chartwell and spend many hours with them both, and when Clementine was ill was especially attentive to Winston, whose flagging interest in life he would try to revive by bringing photographs to jog his memory of various occasions when they had both been together.

In September, 1963, I was as usual away with my family, and Monty made a particular point of paying a visit to Chartwell, reporting to me afterwards:

Things are not too good here. Winston is improving . . . But as you know, he can't now read a book or a paper; he just lies all day in bed doing nothing.*

This has been a great strain on Clemmie, and she finally collapsed under it all and took her bed . . . She really is worn out.

Since I have been here I have been with him all day, trying to interest him in things and showing him photographs of us two in the war. He is now definitely on the mend. He will recover. My view is that Clemmie is now the problem; she is worn out and needs rest. I will come here as much as possible.

One last happy occasion I recall was on 1 April, 1964. It was Clementine's 79th birthday. By now Christopher and I had moved to a larger house near Tunbridge Wells, about half an hour's drive from Chartwell. Winston and Clementine brought Monty, who was staying with them, over to us for luncheon. With our children and one or two close friends and

---

* This was a particularly bad patch. Winston, like many old people, varied in his form; he was certainly not bed-bound generally.

relations who lived nearby we had a happy celebration; but I am so glad I didn't know it was to be my father's and Monty's last visit to us. That October, when Winston left Chartwell to "winter" in London, as was now their wont, it was to be for ever. Winston died peacefully after a fortnight's illness on 24 January 1965, in his 91st year.

Monty himself, in the winter of 1964, was ill and had been through an operation in November. My mother had sent him roses, and in his letter thanking her he says he is looking forward to spending Christmas with them.

When Winston died, Monty was on the high seas, bound for South Africa, where he, in these latter years, used to spend much of the winter. And so he was not able to be present at the great State Funeral which was accorded to my father. Had he been there, he was to have been one of the pall bearers.

After Winston's death, Monty remained a faithful friend to Clementine, visiting her quite often at her new home in Prince's Gate, Kensington. The last letter I had from him was written after one such visit. I was living in Brussels at that time, where Christopher was then a Vice-President of the European Commission. Monty wrote on 8 August, 1966:

My dear Mary,

I had tea with Clemmie in her flat last week and reckoned she wasn't looking too well. She was clearly very tired, and admitted being so. However at her age [81] I suppose that has to be expected.

He then continued to say he would like to see his godson, Jeremy (now fourteen and at Eton). He ended his letter:

I hope you are well. I keep on an even keel myself, my only trouble being that one doesn't get any younger – I will be 80 next year!

For the last years of his life Monty lived in retirement at Isington Mill, the mists of evening closing too around him. He died at the end of March, 1976. On 1 April, her own 91st birthday, Clementine attended her and Winston's great old friend's moving and magnificent Military Funeral at St George's Chapel, Windsor. It was quite a long and tiring event for a very old lady. I accompanied her and wheeled her in her chair to her seat in the chancel. Her eyesight was now very bad, and she could hardly make out the coffin, with Monty's famous beret placed on top; nor could she hear the liturgy and the stirring, beautiful anthem taken from John Bunyan's account of Mr Valiant for Truth's passing through the great river of death: "And all the trumpets sounded for him on the other side" – how fit those words seemed that day. Clementine was nearing the end of her own journey; in twenty months more she too would "yield to the night". But there she was on this cold, grey day – for Winston, and for herself. It had been a great friendship.

A Second Home in France

Alan Breitmeyer

Brigadier A. N. BREITMEYER *was born in 1924 and served with the Grenadier Guards in NW Europe from 1944–1945. He was Adjutant of the 3rd Battalion in Palestine from 1946–1948 and was ADC to Montgomery from 1948–1950. After commanding the 2nd Batallion from 1964–1966, he was Colonel of the Grenadier Guards from 1966–1969 and retired from the Army in 1974. He is a farmer and a member of the Cambridgeshire County Council.*

It was in November, 1948, that the Adjutant of 3rd Battalion, Grenadier Guards, serving in Malaya during the Emergency, and after a Sunday curry lunch in Kuala Lumpur, was awakened by the Chief Clerk. He was given a signal saying that he was to hand over his duties forthwith, and was posted to Paris as ADC to Field-Marshal Montgomery. This was quite a shock to the system under the conditions in which the Battalion was serving at the time under canvas in the steamy heat of Malaya, and it took some time to digest the implications. The somewhat cryptic signal gave little inkling of what the posting was all about, and what my duties would be. I handed over in two or three days and was allotted a priority seat on an RAF plane returning from Singapore.

Having reported to Regimental Headquarters I found out a little more about the posting, and next day went to Dover House in Whitehall, which was to be the London HQ of Monty in his capacity as Chairman of the new Western Europe Commanders-in-Chief Committee, having left the War Office a short time before. I had never met the Field-Marshal and wondered with not a little trepidation whether my rather scanty knowledge of French, up to School Certificate standard, was going to be discovered very rapidly, and whether I could come up to the expectations which were likely to be required. I had one advantage in that I had been at Winchester with Monty's son, and so there was at least some connection with which to break the ice. In fact French hardly came into the interview. Knowing what I later came to know, he was not himself in a position to test me in any way, and after some discussion regarding my career in my Regiment so far, he seemed satisfied that I had the right background.

At this juncture, it is necessary to outline the Defence Organization which had been established with Monty at its head at this time, as it is probably the least publicized and least documented part of his career. The Berlin blockade had only recently been lifted, and it was clear that some form of peacetime military co-operation between the Nations of the West was going to become essential in the future. The OEEC and Schumann Plan for coal and steel had already come into being, and a military set-up was quick to follow under a Benelux umbrella. This was to be headed by the Western Union Chiefs of Staff (WUCOS) and at that time did not include America or Italy, or, of course, Western Germany, which for the time being had no defence forces of its own. Under the Chiefs of Staff there was established the Western Europe Commanders-in-Chief Committee. The Field-Marshal was to be the Chairman, with a small HQ of his own, and two separate HQs for Land Forces and Air Forces established under a French Commander-in-Chief and a British Commander-in-Chief respectively. In addition, there was to be a Naval Liaison Staff, although there were not at that time any Naval Forces specifically allotted to the command of the Commanders-in-Chief Committee. The Land Force HQ (UNITER) and Air Force HQ (UNIAIR) were both at Fontainebleau. Monty's HQ was divided between Dover House in London and a small liaison and co-ordinating staff of about ten officers at Fontainebleau alongside the other Headquarters. The staffs were composed of British, French, Netherlands, Belgian, and Luxemburg officers in rough proportion to the strength of the forces which were allocated under Command. The only American officers were observers, and for this purpose we had two Lieutenant-Colonels who on paper were part of the Graves Registration Unit which was operating from just outside Fontainebleau at the time. The Commander-in-Chief of the Land Forces was General (subsequently Maréchal) de Lattre de Tassigny, and the Air Force Commander was Air Chief Marshal Sir James Robb. The senior Naval liaison officer was Vice-Admiral Jaujard of the French Navy. An emblem was devised to reflect the Alliance, consisting of a gold chain circle of five links on a blue ground, which was flown at Monty's HQ and on his personal car standard.

And what of Monty's position within this organization? It was the first time that an allied planning and command organization had been established in peacetime. He had been used to commanding a multi-national force, both in North Africa and in North-West Europe, and indeed there had been representatives from many countries on his staff. However, it was a very different matter to weld such an organization together in peacetime. National susceptibilities and jealousies were very soon apparent; it was made clear from the outset that it was not considered acceptable to have a Supreme Commander, and his title was therefore Chairman of a Commander-in-Chief's Committee. This irked Monty considerably, and, coupled with the language problem, developed into serious differences of viewpoint with some of his other commanders. From the outset he felt that it was a "complete nonsense" – to use one of his favourite expressions – to try and carry out much planning without bringing West German Forces into the organization, and also without being able to make full use of the massive American Forces which were still deployed in Germany. The latter was probably an easier problem to overcome, since much planning could go on behind the scenes, although America was not at that stage a member of the Western Europe Alliance. The position of Germany, so soon after the war, was naturally something which could not be resolved for some years, but it must have been to Monty's satisfaction that the resurrection of German Armed Forces did come about, through his insistence, at a fairly early stage after the formation of NATO in 1951.

He also found it difficult and frustrating to deal with representatives of nations consisting of so many factions, particularly amongst the French, which could not be expected entirely to pull together. The tragedies of 1940, and the subsequent division of France during the war, had not been overcome in just a few years, and there were at the time, in 1948, elements who had fought for the Free French, some who had been involved with the Maquis, and others who had been in Occupied France, or had been prisoners of war in Germany.

In addition to the small liaison Headquarters in Fontainebleau, headed by Brigadier John Dalton, Monty was allotted a residence by the French Government for his personal use. I well remember the occasion when I was instructed by the London Headquarters to go and reconnoitre the place with a view to getting the Staff established before his first visit a couple of weeks later. This was the Château de Courances, about fifteen miles to the west of Fontainebleau in very pleasant country just outside the forest. I was left speechless on turning the corner in the village to find myself facing an enormous and very beautiful Château at the end of a magnificent avenue of plane trees. It was, and still is, the family home of the Marquis de Ganay (it is now open to the public), and it is of interest that it figures in Robert Lacey's book *Aristocrats* for which the de Ganays were chosen as being representative of the noble families of France. Monty had also been given a French ADC whom I had met the week before. He was Commandant Comte Jean Costa de Beauregard (subsequently retired as a Général de Division), and Monty could not have asked for a nicer companion during his time in France, as Jean Costa had been French instructor at the RMC Woolwich before the war, and spoke the most perfect English. He had also been serving in the personal Cabinet of General de Lattre and General de Gaulle, and knew all the national figures in France and the ins and outs of the government ministries in Paris.

Monty was invited to take over the major part of the Château while the family lived in a wing at one end. It was a most palatial residence, far grander than anything to which he had been accustomed or occupied during the war, and he was also given the staff to run it from the French Armed Services. All the fine furniture, much of it 18th century, remained in situ, and the decor in the bedrooms was sumptuous, with painted panelling of La Fontaine fables, and other fine carving. The bathrooms were, if not 18th century, certainly pre-1900! Some of the baths were made of zinc, and others were perched on pedestals up two steps. They were very deep, held vast quantities of water, and the plumbing arrangements were scarcely up to scratch if many people were staying at one time.

Cutlery, glass and china had to be provided from outside. The problem was overcome very rapidly when an enormous lorry arrived from the French Ordnance Services containing some huge black fitted trunks. These must have originally been taken to the Crimean campaign by the Commander-in-Chief and were fitted with everything which one could possibly require from silver plates to silver entrée dishes and candelabra. The stage was now set for his arrival at what was going to be his part-time home for a number of years to come, both as Chairman of the Committee and later as Deputy Supreme Commander Europe.

On arrival he met the staff, consisting of a French Petty Officer Chef, a Petty Officer Maitre d'Hotel, and five young French airmen and soldiers. There were also his British Military Police who did guard duties at the Château, and his Rifleman Orderly and RASC Driver. I was also allotted my own Guardsman Orderly. So it made a good polyglot collection from different services and regiments, but all got on very well together. I sensed that he was going to enjoy his new home, was going to make the most of it, and meet his obligations to have a number of guests and carry out a certain amount of entertaining. It was made quite clear that he would like to entertain there, rather than giving people dinner in Paris or elsewhere, and the first thing which I had to do was to instal an English billiard table. The purpose of this was not so much to play on it himself, although he was persuaded to do so on one or two occasions, but to have something which would entertain his friends, and thus he would not feel that he must himself stay up late after dinner. It seemed to be a fairly tall order when I received the call from London to "go and find a billiard table" in France. However, my luck was in as the Officers' Club in Paris which had been open since the war was about to close. There was a full-size billiard table there, and with much help from a firm in Paris which Jean Costa managed to dig out, and also help from the French Army Service Corps, the operation was carried out to dismantle and remove the table weighing several tons during one day. It was with a sigh of relief that at eleven o'clock that night I rolled the first ball across it. Master was due to arrive the next day.

Monty had his own DC3 aircraft and VIP crew and so used to come across to France regularly, sometimes for a couple of nights, sometimes for two weeks. He liked to work almost entirely at Courances in the quiet of his study looking over the Le Nôtre garden. His Chief of Staff, General David Belchem, would come out to see him frequently, and if David Belchem was away elsewhere the BGS from Fontainebleau would come to brief him. He very rarely went to the HQ in Fontainebleau, and in fact, I can only recall his going there on one or two occasions in the two years when I served with him. He did not like Paris either, but he had to go there on occasions to meet General de Lattre on his own ground, and sometimes to confer with the British Ambassador, Sir Oliver Harvey (later Lord Harvey). I used to act as courier between the Château and the Headquarters, and many of the Commanders-in-Chief meetings were held at the Château, followed by a lunch party.

He was frequently asked to address conferences, or gatherings of officers at various military Colleges and Headquarters. After a general briefing on the subject and type of audience, he would write all the speeches in his own hand. There were no ghost writers, and the clarity of his English, with no long words and no unnecessary verbiage, and the logic of what he was expressing, made very compelling reading. There was, deliberately, no clerical staff at the Château, so that he could really regard this as a private home where he could relax and entertain, surrounded by the minimum of personal staff. I was the fortunate one in being the link between him and the HQ and was therefore privileged to have a first sight of his instructions and speeches, although the former, as at his Tac HQ in wartime, were nearly always verbal. Endless trouble was taken to get the emphasis and impact just right, and one could see the sometimes repeated erasures of sentences and revision in his very clear hand. Some would say that he over-simplified. I do not believe that this was so in his unanswerable logic in tackling a problem. Where he may have oversimplified was in his unwillingness, or inability, to appreciate national pride and susceptibilities, and consequent strong views of some with whom he had to deal. As a result he tended to brush aside such views and cause resentment.

He took on the part of "*Le Grand Seigneur*" with some relish, and there were frequent visits by senior officers from the Occupied Zones in Germany, and from the other Benelux countries. Whoever was staying the routine would be much the same, and after dinner he would say, "Well I'm off to bed now and you can do what you like. See you in the morning." He had not changed that much from his days as a rather ascetic figure during the campaigns in North Africa and North-West Europe. He preferred to give lunch parties, and, in addition, each year there would be a grand Garden Party on the lawns of the Château, when everybody would be invited from Government Ministers in Paris down to staff captains from all nations in the HQs at Fontainebleau. He really enjoyed these, and used to like circulating round pointing out the glories of the avenues and *"miroirs d'eau"*.

He regarded Courances very much as his second home and he liked having a number of private guests to stay; these included former members of his personal staff, Kit Dawnay and Freddie de Guingand, his stepson John Carver and his cousin Mabel Lunn, as well as many others. He greatly enjoyed the relaxation from more serious military discussions and loved to throw a fly on the water and set an argument going on such subjects as whether or not the French could be considered a logical nation; or for my benefit, whether the Brigade of Guards were better than other Regiments! These friendly arguments would sometimes be carried on for a whole meal. During these he would generally remain silent with a quiet chuckle, but at the end would have the last word and pull the logic of the discussion together rather like an instructor with a syndicate at the Staff College. Once one got to know him and one had his trust he could not have been a more delightful person to serve. He left everyone on his personal staff to get on with their work, to use their imagination, and he was always there to ask for advice when wanted. But you had to be quite sure that you knew what you were talking about, or his very quick and perceptive brain would soon find out the weaknesses in one's argument. He did not drink any spirits, and little wine, except out of politeness, or care about food to the extent of being any sort of gourmet, and one had to strike a balance between keeping menus simple, but at the same time providing a meal which his French visitors would consider worthy of his position, and indeed satisfying to their national palate. He recognized this; it all seemed to work well and to everyone's satisfaction. He gave one complete freedom, took no hand in the arrangements, and it was all scrupulously accounted for to George Cole, his Military Assistant in London (the late Lieutenant-General Sir George Cole), who would keep a close eye on matters for Master.

Not only was he determined to enjoy his home and see some of his friends in these surroundings, but he also liked to be seen in the local countryside. It was perhaps a pointer to that period later in life when he was to set himself up as a kind of unofficial roving Ambassador. During the summer evenings we used to go with the French ADC on walks through the villages and would meet all the locals outside their shops and houses. He liked to talk to them and subsequently entertained many of them to parties in the gardens of the Château, but the French ADC always had to interpret as his knowledge of French was quite abysmal. This lead to one or two rather embarrassing situations, the worst of which was when he invited the local Curé to dine. The latter was quite overcome with this invitation and was somewhat shy, as could be expected, and Monty, in order to break the ice. Described how he visited all the shops and pubs in the villages, Jean Costa, without thinking, translated *"Le Maréchal visite toutes les maisons publiques"* at which the Curé nearly disappeared under the dining table. On one other occasion, when Admiral Jaujard had come to lunch, Monty arrived rather late from an engagement in Paris, and rushed into the room, feeling rather hungry, and exclaimed *"Pardon mon Amiral, j'ai beaucoup de femmes"*. The Admiral, who was somewhat of a Puritan, looked extremely shocked until the French ADC stepped in to correct the grammar and pronunciation. However, this was not the end. He then offered the Admiral a cigarette and followed it with the remark: *"Je ne suis pas un fumier"* (muck heap)!

One of the purposes of his visits to France was to use the Château as a base from which to tour various military establishements and operational units in the Benelux countries. He much enjoyed going off with the French ADC, if the visit was in France, to see units such as the Chasseurs Alpins in the Alps, or a French Air Force base somewhere in the South of France, and he would generally stay with a family who owned a Château or Manoir close by, amongst whom Jean Costa seemed to have innumerable contacts. He made much use on these occasions of his personal aircraft and crew, landing at some very small air strips, sometimes only grass. I used to act as courier and go backwards and forwards between Fontainebleau and his next port of call in order to keep him in touch with the Headquarters' planning work. He paid visits to the French and British commands in Germany and unlike his rather strained relations with de Lattre, he got on extremely well with the French Commander-in-Chief, General Koenig, whose HQ was at Baden-Baden. I well remember a most successful visit when an interesting trip was arranged down the Rhine from Strasbourg to Cologne. He also called upon the Ambassadors in Brussels and The Hague, and used to be accompanied by the British Ambassador when he called upon the various national Ministers of Defence. It was after one such visit in the Netherlands that Sir Philip Nicholls, who was then Ambassador, remarked to me that Monty's ability to put across a problem and suggest a logical answer to it was a lesson for any budding young diplomat.

I cannot recall an occasion when he ever went out to a meal in Paris and this was quite foreign to his way of life. If he wished to relax completely and get away from the military life he would either go on holiday to Switzerland, which he invariably did for a month in February, or he would spend the time quietly at his home in England. He did not ski himself but he was very well looked after by his cousins, the Lunn family, at Murren, and Gstaad, and took a suite of rooms or an annexe in one of the major hotels.

The Western Europe Commanders-in-Chief Committee

existed for less than two and a half years before it blossomed forth into NATO in April, 1951. It was the first time that international military co-operation and planning had taken place actively and continuously in peacetime. It was not an easy time for any Allied commanders, and Monty found it very frustrating. He and de Lattre were both intensely egotistic and vain-glorious leaders. There was a marked clash of personalities and it was most noticeable that the French officer whom he liked most, and for whom he had most respect, was a very able Director of Plans who spoke perfect English, one Colonel Beauffre. He subsequently rose to the rank of Général d'Armée and commanded the French Forces at Suez in 1956.

The language barrier between Monty and de Lattre was almost complete. There was nothing personal in the antagonism, and as far as Monty was concerned it was probably more a feeling that he was dealing with someone who had little experience of high command in war, and for whom he had little regard militarily. The reputation of de Lattre was based upon the invasion of Southern France, partially by French Forces, in August, 1944. Monty had always regarded this as being a total waste and diversion of effort, which contributed little to operations either in North-West Europe or Italy. De Lattre, however, by 1948 was a national hero, and naturally was extremely touchy over matters affecting national prestige and the use of French Forces in the future. Bad relations and mistrust came to such a head after about twelve months that a private meeting was arranged between the two leaders at the instigation of their Chiefs of Staff. At this meeting Jean Costa did the interpreting and after about half an hour he stood between them pronouncing a blessing like a priest. From then on relations were a good deal better and much more business was achieved.

A very high level exercise was held in 1950 to go over the planning which had taken place, and this was attended by

Ministers of Defence and Chiefs of Staff from all the Allied countries. Among them were Mr Shinwell,* then Secretary of State for War, and Field-Marshal Bill Slim as CIGS. Monty had a high regard for both of them. He had served three Secretaries of State when at the War Office, and in his blunt and pungent manner he used to say that he placed them in three categories. The first could understand but could never make a decision. The second, probably the most dangerous, could not understand the basics of a problem, but was only too ready to make a decision; and the third, Mr Shinwell, he found understanding and appreciative, and a man after his own heart with a clear-minded ability to decide on the next course of action. I was called upon to meet Field-Marshal Slim at Villacoublay when he arrived to stay with Monty. I had never met the great man, and, as always on these occasions, one wondered how one would get on during quite a long car journey. However, I need not have worried, as the car had scarcely moved off before he turned to me and said, "Well, tell me now how are they getting on? What is the form?" This certainly made matters much easier, and there was no wool to be pulled over his eyes. At the end of the exercise Field-Marshal Slim made an address and concluded with the words, "For the love of Mike let's get on with it and sort it out". This was typical of his down-to-earth attitude and totally defeated the simultaneous interpreters who were quite unable to cope with this nuance, and left their listeners with somewhat blank looks on their faces. Thereafter, international relations improved still further and diplomacy played a greater part.

The years 1948–1950 were two fascinating ones in the history of military co-operation and, despite national jealousies, a very considerable foundation was laid for NATO to build on. This was largely due to the clear logic in Monty's mind as to what was required, in particular the re-birth of

* Now Lord Shinwell.

German Armed Forces as early as possible, since it was going to be on their territory that any future conflict would be fought. His HQ as Chairman, split between two countries, was small in numbers and had a difficult task in co-ordinating the planning of all the Ground and Air Force Commands. It was a great privilege to be a member of his personal staff at this time, and to be one of the few links between him and so many other organizations in Paris, London and Fontainebleau.

I had applied, the year before joining him, to be considered for a place at University, when the army began to allow officers to be seconded and become graduates after the war, and thus broaden their outlook. Two years with the Field-Marshal give me a far greater opportunity to do this than any time at University could possibly have done, and I shall always be enormously grateful for the experience.

Monty's Little Swiss Friend

Lucien Trueb

LUCIEN F. TRUEB *was born in 1934 and studied chemical engineering, graduating in physical chemistry at Zürich. He pursued a research career in materials science with the Du Pont company and the University of Denver in the USA. Since 1972 he has been the editor of the science-technology pages of the* Neue Züricher Zeitung.

THE IMPORTANT THINGS in life are usually due to accidents or coincidences. However, my first meeting with Field-Marshal Montgomery at the age of eleven and a half years was a clear case of premeditation. Of course I had never dreamed that this would lead to a rather remarkable friendship and a correspondence which spanned a quarter of a century.

In February, 1946, our family was vacationing in Saanenmoeser (Bernese Oberland) and I had just spent another morning receiving group instruction on the fine points of "stemm-christiania" and other then ultra-modern skiing techniques. When I came home for lunch at our rented chalet, my sister excitedly told me that the great Field-Marshal Montgomery had just arrived and would spend some time at the venerable Hotel Golf & Sport. I decided right away that this was a golden opportunity for finally seeing one of the great Allied generals who had so roundly beaten the detested Germans half a year ago.

It must be explained here that Swiss neutrality during the Second World War was certainly the official policy, but it was rather obvious on whose side the sympathies of the great majority lay. The important newspapers openly endorsed the Allied cause, and in the French-speaking part of Switzerland where I grew up, France was considered as a sort of mother-country, at least culturally. At school, the French freedom-fighters were our great heroes; for a time I was infected by this and wanted to be an "FFI" myself. So I built a wooden rifle, equipped myself with a tricolour armband and a beret, happily shooting imaginary "Boches" in the garden. Later on I became aware of the fact that the war was really being fought by British armies and the much more remote Americans and Russians. So, at about age nine, I began to devour the newspapers and followed the fronts with pins on the maps I had put up in my bedroom.

This was the time of the Eighth Army's spectacular campaign in North Africa, and it thoroughly fascinated me. After a lot of pleading, my father even allowed me to watch the movie about the battle of Alamein. I will never forget the night-scenes with the flashes of fire from the big guns, tanks rushing through the sand-dunes and the Scottish infantry advancing to the tune of the bagpipe. There was no question as to who would be my hero from then on: I had become an enthusiastic fan of the wiry general with the black beret. Obligingly, the papers kept publishing new pictures of him, and I pasted them all over my room. This does not mean that I neglected the Americans: I also had pictures of Eisenhower, Bradley and Patton, but only later, after the Normandy invasion. Nevertheless, Monty seemed to be "more real" than all the other generals, which was certainly due to the skill with which he was able to "sell" himself.

For a pre-teenage boy like myself, the war was a marvellous adventure. I had not the slightest idea of the sheer horror of the battlefield, of men in the prime of their youth being killed by the hundreds and mutilated or wounded by the thousands as a matter of daily routine. At that age, one is not of course capable of a differentiated opinion; the Germans were subhuman beasts by definition, so the more of them that were killed the better it was. Of course there were casualties on both sides, and that was just too bad, but as long as the Allies outkilled their foes by a reasonable margin, there was nothing to worry about in peaceful little Switzerland, in our beautiful old house overlooking Lake Neuchâtel!

Back to Saanenmoeser: I had decided I would find Monty

that afternoon, and it really was easy. I knew that elderly gentlemen would not ordinarily be skiing, but spent their time curling or walking around in a dignified manner. Nobody was pushing the stones on the skating rink, so I started to check on the trails beyond the railroad station. And there he was indeed, stomping around in the snow, illegally wearing a piece of foreign uniform in a neutral country – his black beret. I might not have recognized him otherwise, as I had imagined him to be much taller. So I skied right up to him and said, "*Bonjour, Monsieur*", the way one greeted teachers and other respectable persons. Monty answered something which I didn't understand, but it sounded friendly; so I went along with him for a minute or so and then quietly slipped away. I had not realized that Monty, as he so often did, was posing for a press photographer who was shooting pictures from some distance. Inevitably, I was in the best pictures of the lot: the great Field-Marshal with a cute "native" kid was the perfect subject, so this eventually appeared in many newspapers with the caption "Monty and his little Swiss friend".

Our winter vacation was just about over; when we got home I was madly excited to find myself in such august company, not only in the daily press but also in the window of the local newspaper office. I managed to buy the picture and wanted to send it to the Field-Marshal in order to have it autographed. However, the family – which meant that father was giving orders and everybody agreed – decided that this would have to be done properly. So I wrote the draft of a letter, father edited it carefully and a friend of the family who was an excellent English teacher translated it. Finally, I had to copy the whole thing laboriously, with only a faint idea of what I was doing. Needless to say that I omitted a whole line on the first try and an important word on the second one. Only the third version was deemed acceptable, and with a sigh of relief I surrendered the letter to my mother who artfully wrapped it into a box of chocolates. The whole was then mailed to Gstaad, where Monty was spending the second half of his vacation.

To my indescribable delight, a rather large brown envelope arrived a couple of days later; it contained two photographs and a most friendly thank-you note. The Field-Marshal remembered me indeed and even invited me to come to see him in Gstaad. The photographs were "both taken in Germany before the war ended. The larger one was taken during the Battle of the Ardennes in December, 1944, when it was very cold." Among the hundreds of pictures Monty would eventually send me over the years, this one is still my preferred; it was framed and is now standing on the mantelpiece over the fireplace. I would think it is an unposed snapshot, taken in the woods during the fateful days of the last German offensive. In this picture, Monty is wearing a zippered jacket two sizes too large but padded by several sweaters, a thick woollen scarf and the beret pulled down deep over his forehead. He looks emaciated and tired, but the face radiates immense power, a total determination to win. This called for another letter, which was produced under conditions no less painful than the first time. Since the snowdrops were already blooming in our garden, it was decided that the Field-Marshal might like to have some.

Package number two was mailed to Gstaad and this time the answer came by special delivery. Monty explained that he was just leaving, but would stay for a couple of days in Berne: would I care to come and see him at the British Embassy? No question about that, so father took me to our capital and dutifully dropped me at the gate. I was ushered into a small parlour and Monty joined me right away. He gave me a big hug and had me sit next to him on the sofa. Then he started to ask a great many questions – in French, which he spoke well.* He wanted to know all the details: my family, my school, our

* See, however, p. 104.

house, sports, everything. Did I have a boat? No, I didn't have a boat because my parents thought I would certainly capsize with it. Then did I have a bicycle? Unfortunately I didn't have a bicycle either, as my parents were worried I might break my neck on it. Monty thought that a boy nearly twelve years old really ought to have a bicycle. Maybe I might get one if I promised to ride it very safely? Then he wanted to know the date of my birthday and told me that his birthday was on 17 November. He also asked me to write him on the first of every month from now on and give him all the news. I was dismissed with another fatherly hug.

Back at home I had to give a highly detailed report on my interview with the Field-Marshal. My parents didn't quite know what to think about the whole thing. Had their son possibly fallen into the clutches of some sort of a pervert? A letter came from Headquarters, British Army of the Rhine just in time to reassure them. It said: "I feel I ought to write you regarding the friendship that has grown up between Lucien and myself. I am devoted to children and Lucien reminds me of my favourite brother, the youngest of the family, who died when 12 years old. The likeness is very remarkable; and when I met Lucien in Berne I saw at once the same delightful character."

Everybody familiar with Monty's biography knows that there was indeed such a brother: his name was Desmond. But whether I really looked like him is still an open question. It is probably not very relevant; the main point is that Monty was extremely fond of children, but in a highly selective way. They had to be boys old enough to make sense and admire him without fail, but before the age when they start to question things and develop their own opinions. When this happened, they were gently phased out and eventually replaced; in this manner Monty accumulated about half a dozen young "protégés" in the course of the next twenty years; I had the privilege of being the first of the lot. Yet, they all remained very special to him for the rest of his life: he checked on their progress, wrote to them and kept sending samples of a seemingly endless supply of large-size photographs showing himself on inspection trips all over the world.

Monty returned to his headquarters and our correspondence started in earnest. He declared that we had now become real friends, and that I should write in French until I mastered English well enough, so that I might write more naturally and say things my own way. He must have noticed that every letter I wrote was being thoroughly edited by my father who was a terrible perfectionist in everything related to writing. This early and severe training certainly did me a lot of good and prepared me for my future career as a journalist. At the time though it was a grind; I dreaded the deadline of each new letter to the Field-Marshal and the entire house was in turmoil towards the end of the month. Yet the rewards kept coming: enormous manila envelopes filled with photographs, often autographed or at least bearing handwritten explanations on the back. And his letters, always written in a remarkably neat and firm hand, show a genuine interest in the rather trivial and straightforward life of his little friend. The style was exactly right for a boy of my age; the following excerpt is rather typical. "I had a good journey back to Berlin; I send you a photo taken in the train. I also send you some photos showing my schloss in Germany. It is a lovely house with a big park and we have swans on the lake. I have been in England since I saw you in Berne; I have to go there a good deal and I fly there in my aeroplane." And, nearly a year ahead, plans were being made for the next Swiss vacation; he would be in Gstaad again and wanted me to stay with him for at least a week. I would have to clear this with my parents and the school authorities. Furthermore, he requested a good picture of myself: so I had to go to a professional photographer and endure a whole morning of posing. The picture was duly sent to the War Office and deemed acceptable.

Thus, Monty wrote in May, 1946: "I like the photo very much, and it stands in my bedroom next to the clock; I then see you when I wake up." He also needed a reconfirmation of the date of my birthday, he wasn't sure whether he remembered it correctly (he did), and wanted to send me a nice present.

For a month, everybody in the family tried to guess what the "nice present" would be. First a letter came, obviously written in a hurry; a few days later he wrote again, in his very touching way: "I wrote to you on 28 June, your birthday, by airmail letter. I had only got back from Athens and I wrote at once as I did not want you to think I had forgotten and for you to be disappointed. I love you too much to ever forget. I want to give you a present but do not quite know what to send you. So I am sending you this 20 francs and with it you must buy something for yourself". As the months went by, the greetings in Monty's letters became more and more affectionate. Taken out of context, they may sound like something one would write to a fiancée or mistress, and could easily lead to misinterpretations. Yet, this was just the reflection of a totally straightforward personality, using a highly restricted vocabulary so that everybody would understand him. When he liked somebody, or felt affection or sympathy, it was love; he used the word very liberally, both in English and French.

By November, 1946, detailed plans were made as to my stay in Gstaad three months later. Several letters concentrated on this project; there was just a trip to Moscow to get out of the way, but nothing would interfere with the holidays in Switzerland. And he wrote: "We will go on walks together and I shall hope to improve your English; and you will help me improve my French. I have given up skiing since I broke my back when my aeroplane crashed in Germany in 1945, but you will be able to go skiing with my aides-de-camp".

Those two weeks in Gstaad were a high point of my early youth. Monty was fantastic with children, giving them firm guidance, insisting on strict discipline, yet spoiling them mercilessly, constantly making miracles happen. We were living in the large and beautiful chalet owned by "Donna Guinness" as Monty called her, of beer-brewing fame. It was full of antique furniture, valuable paintings and incredible quantities of knick-knacks, mostly made of coloured glass. What really impressed me though was an old chest in the living-room: it contained a powerful radio and every morning before breakfast we would listen to the news from the BBC.

The ADCs, Noel Chavasse and Pat Hobart, one of Monty's relatives, were great sport; they were young men just over twenty and their skiing was not much better than mine, only a bit faster. Pat had to return to England after a while, as his father was gravely ill. He was replaced by Johnny Henderson. We saw a lot of each other on the slopes and had our little conspiracies to circumvent the strict order of the day which Monty had made up for the entire two weeks. For example we avoided some of the steeper slopes the Field-Marshal had judged to be particularly good for training our skills; he had an uncanny eye for evaluating any kind of terrain, even from great distances. Or instead of walking to the lift station, which was supposed to warm us up, we took one of those horse-drawn sleighs which served as taxis. After a morning of hard skiing we joined Monty at the chalet for lunch. The cook prepared gourmet meals as a matter of routine; not even artfully handwritten menu-cards were missing. Noel and Johnny soon found out that a second dessert could be concocted out of the fruit and coffee courses: mashed bananas with cream and sugar. Monty the ascetic frowned on it and declared it was bad for our health, but the three of us gorged ourselves on this calorie-bomb until we hardly could get up from our chairs. Then one of the ADCs would call the War Office in London and tell their starving colleagues about the terrible time we had digesting those loads of mashed bananas and cream. The standing joke of both ADCs was to turn to me when the Field-Marshal was not looking and whisper, "Lucien, I've eaten too much" and very realistically simulate being sick.

In the afternoon Monty would take a walk; this meant that we first rode the chair-lift to the top of the Wasserngrat where the best slopes of the Gstaad area are located. He would then walk downhill once while I skied the mountain three times, always making a short stop next to him so I could report on how things were going. After my third run Monty had reached the bottom of the hill and we walked home together. He would always wear three or four sweaters to start out, one on top of the other, taking them off as needed. He said that he had learned to do this in the desert, where there are enormous temperature differences between day and night. Tea with light cakes, butter and marmalade was served at five o'clock, and then everybody started to work. The ADCs had their desks where they shuffled papers and made phone-calls. Monty and I retired to a small study where we answered the mail that had accumulated during the day. There were heaps of fan-mail, requests for autographs and many packages. I had to open these and show the contents to the Field-Marshal who decided whether he would write a thank-you note himself or delegate this task to me. We received just about anything one could imagine: brandy, wine and cigars were on top of the list, even though everybody should have known that Monty neither smoked nor drank. Yet, he was quite happy to get such things: he needed them for his guests back home. Then there was often eau-de-cologne, perfumed soaps, boxes of stationery, chocolates and candy, baskets of fruit, even toys. Many manufacturers would send samples of their products, all kinds of funny gadgets like vegetable-peelers or knife-sharpeners. And then there were the amateur woodcarvers, brass-turners and ironsmiths who wanted Monty to have "masterpieces" from their workshops. The ladies on their side had been busy knitting sweaters, gloves and ski-socks for him. I had to write a lot of letters both in French and German to thank the senders. Many of them certainly were disappointed: instead of the hoped-for autograph of the British Field-Marshal, they got the scribblings of a teenage boy! Monty made it a habit to give me a present every day, usually taken from the packages that had arrived; once I even got a ball-pen. They were all the rage then and cost a fortune; mine leaked terribly but I loved it, even though much of the ink eventually ended up on my hands, face and clothes.

Monty took a lot of pictures with his beautiful Rolleiflex – some piece of war-booty from Germany, which I was sometimes allowed to use, so he could pose for me in front of the mountains. He liked to wear the white sheepskin coat he had received as a present from the Swiss Army, and bragged that he now was a Swiss Field-Marshal. The second Swiss Field-Marshal in history was me: Monty decided that I should don his army tunic complete with ten inches of ribbons, and the famous beret, which wasn't even oversize. Those pictures certainly are the funniest ones in my album. After this, any military career could only be anticlimatic; this is probably why I retained the rank of private during my entire period of active army duty!

Dinner always was a formal coat and tie affair and I was too young for that. After the secretarial work was over, I had to take my bath: Monty towelled me off personally so I wouldn't catch a cold. Then I had to put on my pyjamas and robe: I would get a room-service dinner in the Field-Marshal's bedroom, then retired to my own room. Monty always had dinner just with his ADCs; there never were any guests, and true to his legend he went to bed shortly after nine. Sometimes I was still awake and noticed that he would open my door very quietly and check on me with a small flashlight. I always pretended that I was sound asleep. In the meantime Noel and Johnny sneaked out of the house, destination unknown, and invariably came home very late. Monty of course knew about this, as nothing ever escaped his attention; with mock-seriousness he demanded reports on his assistants' nightly activities. Even though my English was still very poor at that time, I did grasp words like bar, drinks and ladies; those "confessions" obviously reinforced the very high opinion the Field-Marshal had about his own, absolutely flawless virtue.

The high point of this vacation was the ski-jumping contest for the Montgomery Cup. The best Swiss jumpers competed, there were hundreds of spectators and the newsreel service filmed it all. We watched from the jury-stand with the mayor, other local notables and the very fat director of the local tourism board. Monty kept kidding him about his enormous weight and there was a lively debate about the conversion of kilogrammes into English stones. In the evening I was allowed to attend the banquet where Monty handed the cup to the winner and made a short speech; he thought ski-jumping was a marvellous test of manliness, as it required both daring and skill, just the qualities good soldiers ought to have. My two weeks were now over: it had been an absolutely glorious time and the tears just streamed down my cheeks when I took leave of the Field-Marshal.

Back home it was the old routines of school and letter-writing: Monty had asked that I should now write bi-monthly; this wasn't as bad as it may sound for by then I had acquired some sort of routine in that task. And his answers were marvellous. Right after Gstaad he wrote, "I miss you here very much. I have given you all my love and you are my very dear little friend. We must both look forward to next February, when we will meet again. The time will soon pass. Au revoir". He now called me "*mon garçon*" and asked me to call him "Papa"; this is the way he signed his letters too, with or even without quotation marks. My father didn't particularly like this, but I found it completely natural to have two daddies. The letters now came at an accelerated rate, almost always accompanied by some small present: photographs, stamps, minor trophies from the war and post-war period. And the big present, which had already been discussed in Gstaad now materialized, a bicycle. I bought exactly the model and make I liked best, and Monty sent the money to pay for it in a plain envelope. He travelled a great deal that year and it was most fascinating for me to hear from such far-away places as Palestine, India, Singapore, Australia and Africa. He actually told me very little about the landscapes; there might be a casual remark about the weather, but his main interest lay in the reception he would get in the cities he visited. Travelling great distances was still almost an adventure in that pre-jet age and he enjoyed it as a kind of sport. A typical letter would say: "Australia is a huge country. On 12 July I flew in my aeroplane from Perth to Sydney: over 2000 miles; we did a non-stop run in 8½ hours with a tail wind of 30 miles an hour".

And already plans were made for the next Gstaad vacation, but I was prepared early for a possible disappointment: travel restrictions had been imposed due to the bad state of the British economy and no money could be taken out of the country. In January, 1948, it became definite: "You must be brave mon Lucien", he wrote: "It is a shattering blow. But we can write each other. And I shall hope for better days in 1949, when I can visit your sunny land again and we can be together once more". Monty spent his vacation in the Channel Islands that year, where he would go for long walks on the beaches. He now decided that it was time for me to start writing in English; I was being privately tutored in that language and with an occasional phone-call to the teacher on some of the finer points of grammar, things worked out reasonably well. As a reward, I kept receiving huge envelopes full of photographs, and also impressive lists of his medals and freedoms;

he remarked that he was a Freeman of thirty-three cities, none of them being in Switzerland! Aside from the press photographs, I would get professionally done pictures which were eventually framed; they decorated my room for many years. One I particularly liked shows him on horseback; he had written on the bottom: "Rommel's white Arab stallion captured by me in Germany and given by me to the King". On my part, I had to send him snapshots so he could check on how I was getting along. Once he commented, "I always study carefully the photos you send me and I compare them with the previous ones. You will soon be grown up and I shall hardly recognize the dear little Swiss boy that I first met in February, 1946."

Preparations soon started for the Field-Marshal's next Swiss vacation. The foreign travel restrictions had been lifted and Monty found out that he could stay at the Murren Palace Hotel as a guest of the owner, Lady Mabel Lunn, who happened to be his cousin. He would spend a week in Gstaad too for the Montgomery Cup jumping competition. This is where I would join him. In the meantime I was put in charge of the correspondence with the tourism authorities and had to settle a number of minor issues.

Monty had then just finished rebuilding and refurbishing Isington Mill in Hampshire, his new country house. Besides, his new duties as deputy chief commander of the NATO forces entitled him to a residence on the Continent, the Château de Courances, in the French département Seine-et-Oise. So plans were also made much beyond Gstaad: I would have to come to see both of his new homes in England and France. Father declared immediately that this was out of the question, but he got upset too soon.

Ebullient as ever, Monty had organized his schedule in our country down to the last minute and wrote, "I want the very best weather and plenty of snow while I am in Switzerland. Please arrange it!! We will have a lovely time at Gstaad and of course you will now stay up and have dinner with us at night".

Things weren't anything like as opulent as they had been two years earlier. The chalet attached to the Park Hotel was much smaller than the Guinness residence and hotel staff serviced it. Besides, Monty had only one ADC this time, a very tall fellow named Andrew Burnaby-Atkins. Yet, we had plenty of fun and skied all day long. There was little fan-mail this time: the war had already become a distant memory and people rapidly forgot about it as well as the generals who had fought it, at least in Switzerland. Outwardly, Monty hadn't changed; he still was the loving father-figure and we went on long walks together. He was greatly interested in my progress at school and how the bicycle was running. It was only a short week, but Monty arranged that I could join him on a visit to the Omega watch-factory just before he left the country. He had been there before, but decided that he hadn't really seen things well enough. The real reason dawned on me later: he had received only a cardboard model of a watch the first time, and his aim was on a self-winding gold Omega. The directors of the company finally got the message and Monty was duly presented with what he had wanted; he was very proud of this new trophy.

The correspondence I received during the following year was still very affectionate, but mostly consisted of directions as to where my letters should be mailed: Monty was constantly on the move between England, France and the other NATO countries. At one time he planned to come to see us at our house, but some political tensions prevented this trip. He was in transit through Switzerland for a few hours in September, 1949, and I joined him for a picnic somewhere in the Jura mountains. Afterwards he wrote: "You are definitely growing up and are no longer a little boy: 16 next year. I often wish you were 12 again!".

The next Swiss vacation was once more to be split between

Murren and Gstaad, and I was to join him at the latter place. The opulence was down another notch, as we stayed in the Park Hotel this time, in a very pleasant suite admittedly. There was no ADC and Monty seemed to be working harder than ever; he would do a lot of writing on the balcony and only occasionally took an afternoon off for a walk. I was now only three years away from the university and rather conceited about being able to read Livy and Ovid in the original Latin. I am also afraid that I started arguments on any subject that came up, whether I knew something about it or not. Monty didn't seem to like this at all and would rapidly cut me off, which I resented. So there was an element of tension between us, even though I tried hard to behave decently. When the week was over and time came to say goodbye, Monty told me that we now should have a gap; I didn't understand the word and had to check it in the dictionary back home. In the next letter he explained further: "The relationship cannot be same as when you were a little boy . . . Now we need a gap during which you will become a young man. You can visit me again when you are 18." Furthermore, three letters a year were deemed enough: Easter, midsummer and his birthday. Monty now signed with his full name again, and for several years his letters were much on the same pattern: he was constantly travelling and enjoined me to work very hard at school. He kept an affectionate and lively interest in what I was doing, especially when military duty started for me and I began to travel abroad in my early college years. One of his typical statements reads: "You can only reach worthwhile objectives in life by hard work and devotion to duty: which I am sure you realize".

About a dozen letters Monty wrote me between 1955 and 1960 were lost in a fire that broke out in the house where I lived while working for a degree in chemical engineering at the technical university in Zurich. Eight months ahead of time he invited me for lunch in Murren in February, 1956; this was

Lucien F. Trueb

the last time I would see him. He was nearly seventy then, but still the old steel-wire bundle, bouncing with energy. I had to give him a detailed report on the doctoral thesis I had started, but otherwise Monty kept talking, mostly about himself. I proudly told him about my Volkswagen, but he wasn't interested: he thought that Britain was making the best cars in the world and that sooner or later I would graduate to the Rolls-Royce, which was his favorite. The walk we took through the village was a real military inspection: the clothes people had hung out to dry, the snow-heaps along the road, the piles of firewood in front of the houses were meticulously checked for rectilinear alignment. Empty cigarette-packs and dog-excrement were catapulted out of the way with an expert stroke of his cane. And then he proved to me that his hearing, eyesight and general physical fitness were much superior to mine. I was dismissed with another lecture on the importance of hard work.

After graduating from college I went to live in the United States for many years; the correspondence with the Field-Marshal then continued on a yearly basis. I would write to him for his birthday, the answer invariably came just a few days later, generally dated November 17. In those late letters, Monty became philosophical. When I began to think of returning to Switzerland, but was undecided, he wrote: "One's own country always calls. I have seen most countries in the world but am always glad to get back to England – which I reckon is the best, in spite of its climate!" In 1965 he wrote: "I keep very well. But one doesn't get any younger. In two years I will be 80". And in 1968: "My doctors will no longer allow me to go to Switzerland because of the heights, so I have become a sea-level person." A year later he commented: "I am getting old – 82 – and am beginning to feel my age. I now live a very quiet life, and my travelling days are over. But I am very happy and my friends come and see me."

The last letter I received from Monty is dated 20 November,

1970, and is worth being quoted fully, as it was a kind of farewell-message. It says: "Dear Lucien: I was glad to hear from you and to learn the news. It always gives me great pleasure when boys I have known climb to great heights and succeed in life. This you have done and I congratulate you. You deserve success since you have worked hard. I hope you will climb ever higher. Good luck to you. Yrs. sincerely Montgomery of Alamein".

Then it was silence; I kept writing faithfully, always in November, but there were no more answers. I learned much later that Monty had suffered a heart attack in 1970, from which he never really recovered, even though he lived for another six years. In fact, the writing had become a bit shaky in his last letter, even though it was still the unmistakable and beautifully legible hand.

Sons of the Clergy

Richard Luckett

Dr RICHARD LUCKETT *was born in 1945. He was a Lecturer at the Royal Military Academy in 1967. He is a University Lecturer in English at Cambridge University, having been a Fellow and Dean of St Catharine's College 1969–1977 and since 1977 a Fellow of Magdalene College and Pepys Librarian.*

IT BEGINS IN my memory with reading Genesis III 8–19 at a service of Lessons and Carols in Pluckley Church. The effect a little frightened me; I could hear how high and apart my voice sounded and sensed, dimly, that in this exploitation of a presumptive innocence to recount such a story, there was a theatricality beyond the dreams of six-year-old exhibitionism. Afterwards Major Reynolds told me I had read well, my first certain recollection of him, though I remember how on another occasion he peered round the door of my room when he came for supper at the Rectory and I had been put early to bed.

I had started at the village school; this was not a success. I learned little except for an extensive scatological vocabulary, and was puzzled by the effect this produced on the Mothers' Union. Father approached Major Reynolds to ask if I could attend Northaw, just a mile and a half away, as a day boy, not realizing that the Reynolds only accepted boarders. There was no question of managing the boarding fees. On learning this Tom Reynolds offered to make it possible.

Such generosity must have been one of the qualities that commended him to Montgomery. Tom Reynolds – "T.R." to Northaw boys – had left the army with a vocation to be a preparatory schoolmaster. His attitudes were summed up in two sermons he preached to us shortly before his death, one on the injunction, "Constantly speak the truth, boldly rebuke vice", the other on a phrase he loathed, "I couldn't care less". His bearing was erect, his eyes were bright, his uniform a brown or green velvet jacket, a thumbstick, and an ancient but elegant hat.

Bernard Montgomery's friendship with Tom and Phyllis Reynolds began in India and culminated in their guardianship of his son David during the war. It was brought home to me in its domestic aspect when Phyllis Reynolds, who had been spring-cleaning, came into a dormitory at Norman Court one evening with a workbasket and said "Quiz?". It was a cornucopia of Royal Warwickshire badges, shoulder straps, pips and medal ribbons, evidence of years of devoted sewing.

Montgomery was a presence, but not a very immediate one, to a new boy at Surrenden Dering, the Caroline manor (much of it in fact Victorian) in Pluckley parish where, with his son-in-law Richard Lewis, T.R. had recently returned to schoolmastering. The Field-Marshal had visited Surrenden, and come to matins at Pluckley Church (though I have no recollection of this), but his true tutelary emanation was symbolic; my first dormitory was *Alamein*, and though battles of the Hitler war in which Montgomery had not participated were similarly commemorated, those in which he had played the preponderant part (including even Arnhem) seemed to matter most.

Surrenden was gutted by fire on Friday 10 October, 1952. The school moved, with remarkable speed and smoothness, to Norman Court, West Tytherley, on the borders of Hampshire and Wiltshire. The strain must have done much to bring on Tom Reynolds's death not long afterwards. It was all very different from Surrenden: great beech woods, yews, the soil chalky and flinty. The woods attracted thunderstorms, and for some reason, perhaps simply proximity to Isington Mill, Montgomery seemed much closer.

I did not then appreciate the awful eminence of a Field-Marshal, though Letts pocket diary intimated that such officers were paid £10 a day, with allowances, for life, which compared favourably with my termly ten shillings pocket money. I supposed that all Field-Marshals drove cars with windscreens that sloped the wrong way; other boys took a more informed interest, but, since my parents had no car, automobiles were not devices to which I was prepared to devote attention.

The Reynolds and Lewis families contrived to run Northaw as a combination of private school and country house. This they could do because they chose to keep numbers low and not to admit day boys. Richard Lewis's labrador loped around the school, as did, much less liked, Phyllis Reynolds's cairns. Flint-picking was a regular activity, and potato-picking a seasonal one, for the whole school. Privileged boys acted as Richard Lewis's beaters, drove the tractor, or rode the pony. The excellent library had a good stucco ceiling and, let into stucco frames, a fine set of paintings by Jan Weenix. The dining room had ceiling frescoes in the manner of Angelica Kauffmann. Guests of the family ate at top table at breakfast and lunch, and at first there seemed little to choose (save a missing eye and arm), in the category of military men, between Field-Marshal Montgomery and General Carton de Wiart, or two other regular visitors, one of whom came to fish for trout, the other to exercise his passion for lopping trees, often bringing himself down with the branch. What gradually differentiated the Field-Marshal for me was the proliferating display of photographs of him and his activities on corridor and dormitory walls and, more pleasurably apprehensible, periodic showerings of Swiss chocolate. This was what the Field-Marshal thought or knew that boys liked. It came in three forms: Toblerone; bears which were inexpressibly Swiss and posed agonising problems of equitable division; and bright military drums, filled with chocolate coins in gold foil. These comprehensively distinguished the splendour of the Field-Marshal, as did the fact that he alone was allowed to swell our fixed weekly dispensation of sweets with such largesse.

I did not know at the time, nor did anyone else in the school besides the Reynoldses and Lewises, that Montgomery's pride in his parentage and consequent interest in the sons of the clergy had taken practical expression in provision for the education of a chosen boy at St John's School, Leatherhead, of which he was now Chairman of the Governors. The Reynoldses and Lewises had extended their generosity to others besides my parents and a natural progression from Northaw to St John's was established. It was because of this that in 1955, aged nine, I made my closer acquaintance with the Field-Marshal. I must have been called up to speak to him when he visited, for I remember a sensation of tongue-tiedness that never really left me in his company. The conversation of Field-Marshals, it appeared, was unprecedentedly laconic and interrogative; a response less laconic seemed uncalled for, yet as laconic, even if feasible, rude. I was equally disconcerted by the fierce brilliance of his eyes and his resolute substitution of "w"'s for "r"'s. A school friend suffered much criticism from Phyllis Reynolds for doing just this, but Field-Marshals were obviously exempt. My own first conscious realization that I was in a special position with regard to the Field-Marshal came when Mrs Reynolds rebuked me for saying 'Montgomery' with the first 'o' short and unprefixed by his title. It was something, she told me, that I of all people should get right.

The invitation to visit him came formally to me, though there must have been another letter to my parents. Preparations were put in hand, a new sponge-bag bought, I was enjoined to keep my clothes neat, and mother took me up to London, third-class, and put me on the Alton train, travelling first-class. For years I thought this transfer symbolic of genteel poverty and its concern with appearances, but I now see that a child travelling alone was more wisely placed in a first-class carriage. The Field-Marshal was waiting for me on the platform, and his driver wafted the armoured Rolls to

Isington. As we drove in I saw a group of young men in shirt-sleeve order sitting in the sun on the wall by the mill stream. One had a rifle; they were looking into the water and laughing. I must have asked what they were doing. The Field-Marshal replied, "Shooting trout," then added with relish, "Some people wouldn't think it sporting." He sounded dismissive of "some people" and asked the soldier-servants (of whom he seemed to have a number) "what the bag was".

Then there was a bemusing tour of the Mill and caravans. The caravans came as a surprise – mechanical monsters at the bottom of the garden. My experience of holidaymakers on the Folkestone road had not prepared me for these vast trailers. I loved the house with its polished wood floors, rugs and plain panelling, and the impression of light and spaciousness, despite the lowish ceilings. Everything that could be was built in, and I decided (perhaps the chocolates played their part) that it was rather Swiss. I had not before seen so many pictures of one man in one place. That which I immediately admired was by Salisbury, for the reason that when its subject stood in front of it the excellence of the likeness was remarkable. I said so, and it was the first time that any observation of mine had given Montgomery perceptible pleasure. The other notable thing about the house was the number of silver and gold caskets, some with surprising animals on top. They held, Montgomery explained, the liberties of the cities of which he was a freeman. They seemed to be everywhere. There was not an abundance of military trophies, though I was as much excited by a ceremonial *Kukri* as I was uncomprehending of the Luneburg surrender document.

Tea struck me as on the frugal side, but this, it transpired, was because I was to have dinner, a meal which, in its evening manifestation, I had otherwise experienced only on Christmas day. When dinner came it also proved to be the first time I had been waited on in a private house. Between tea and dinner we watched television, which we did not have at home, as the Field-Marshal had evidently gathered. Dinner I can remember well; there were candles and silver on the brilliantly polished table, and we ate fish, young potatoes and peas, fruit salad and brandysnaps, the latter intensifying for me the Christmas confusion. But of what was said I am less certain, though the Field-Marshal certainly embarked on one set piece, an exuberant account of how he had won a Flying Fortress as a result of a bet with an American general who had been so foolish as not to restrict the terms of the wager. It seemed a case of winner take all. It caused me to reflect that I was glad not to have been the American, and that I could not have got away with that kind of thing at Northaw. I thought it a pity that he had not kept the plane rather than the caravans, but could quite see that there was nowhere to put it; the caravan sheds took up quite enough space anyway. I was sent to bed early on the grounds that I must have been tired by the journey. The Field-Marshal came in to see that I was established and, exclaiming "But you must have a good book" (I had several in my suitcase), produced from the low range of shelves *Eric, or Little by Little*, explaining that not only was it a good book, but it had been written by his grandfather. It was in an embossed cover and contained vivid engravings. I was fascinated and mystified from the first page. I thought it was probably about the sin against the Holy Ghost, on the grounds that the sin was both perturbing and inexplicable, as also was whatever *Eric* was about. Life at Northaw was distinctly different, though I gathered that the Field-Marshal did not think so. Later he came in to discover why my light was still on, after which I put it off and exorcised the horrors of *Eric* by listening to the wind in the oaks and the tumble of the mill race outside.

I can recall that first day of my first stay, but after that occasions merge. One Sunday (my visits were at weekends, and I knew that the Field-Marshal could scarcely abide Saturday and Sunday, and longed for Monday) we did not go to church – an omission that much impressed me; at home and at Northaw services were obligatory. I began to see virtues in being a Field-Marshal. On another occasion, however, we went to matins in Winchester Cathedral, where the Field-Marshal was duly met and escorted by the vergers to a stall in the choir. I wondered if God minded the defective "r"'s in the Field-Marshal's crisply uttered prayers and responses.

On the evening of the second day we sat and leafed through what seemed vast albums of cartoons; he had, he said, collected every one that represented him, whether sympathetically or not. It was a peculiar sensation. At home we took *The Times*. At Northaw there would be *The Times* and *The Telegraph* in the library. *The Telegraph* printed cartoons, I think, but they had no interest for me. The world of the popular press was quite new to me, with the result that whilst the Field-Marshal derived vast amusement from these representations, my reaction was of incomprehension and shock that the small, neat, almost super-humanly compact figure next to me should be allowed to acquire, in these depictions, a monstrously twisting proboscis and impossibly baggy battle-dress. My reaction also reflected my real ignorance as to how Montgomery had mastered both the battlefield and the press.

On the Monday we drove to London, the occasion providing the opportunity for an exposition of the full glories of the Rolls; the built-in aircraft compass for desert navigation, the map table, the internal telephone for the driver, the power-assisted steering and windows, the compartments for weapons, its unquenchable and historic capacity for petrol. 'No cocktail bar, though,' announced the Field-Marshal. In London, before the driver took me on to Waterloo and the Pluckley train, I was taken to see the CIGS's office in the Horse Guards. The saluting and coming-to-attention was prodigious. Once there I was asked if I wanted to spend a penny: "Always best to, if you can." I did. "It's at the end of the corridor." I walked in the direction indicated. Half-way along the corridor stood a pair of sentries. As I passed them they solemnly presented arms. It was a compliment I could not conceive how to return. I continued on my errand, feeling a very small boy indeed, and dreading the return journey. So far as I could see, the soldiers guarded only the lavatory.

But I did not leave the Horse Guards diminished, for on the desk were gifts: a photograph of the Field-Marshal, not in uniform, but in a white fur overcoat at Mürren; a copy of translations from Hans Anderson by M. R. James ("the best man," the Field-Marshal said; I did not know, but it promised to be a welcome change from *Eric*, which continued to haunt me long after my stay was over); a Swiss perpetual calendar with a picture of William Tell, and, inevitably, a drum of chocolate coins. Ranked in my bedroom at home they were tangible evidence that the Field-Marshal had advanced into my territory.

A correspondence followed. The envelopes were of a distinctive weight and shape, and often addressed in a distinctive green ink. The letters themselves were brief, but never failed to contain a new 10s or even £1 note. The difficulty was to answer them; they had precisely the same effect as the Field-Marshal's conversation (at least as it occurred until one had been alone with him several hours). Indeed after that first visit I spent hours at the kitchen table, under the eye of my mother, struggling with what obviously had to be a model thank-you letter, and obstinately refused to become one. It was no easier to answer a letter which ran:

My dear Richard,
   I send you this £1 as a Christmas present. You may find some good use for it in the holidays. I shall hope to see you at Northaw in March when I am going to see the Boxing.
   My love to you.
                              Yours sincerely,
                              Montgomery of Alamein.

The best use that I could think of for the £1 was to get me out of the boxing, which was compulsory, at which I was hopeless, and which I loathed. But it could not be spent this way, and I had March, and an inevitable bloody nose, looming for the next two months.

Sometimes I managed momentarily to rise to the occasion. In February of 1957 the Field-Marshal wrote from the Palace Hotel, Mürren, saying:

> I was glad to hear from you and to learn that you are now in the V Form. That is good.

But the encouragement could not outweigh the gloom induced by the second paragraph.

> I hope you will have a good term. Work hard and finish up Head Boy before you leave.

I knew myself, and Northaw, well enough to recognize that that was something that I could never be.

My next visit to Isington I recall less clearly. I set out, not from Pluckley, but from our holiday at Upnor, where Father was acting as *locum tenens* for the parish and the TS *Arethusa*. Bad weather made it a poor time for the rest of the family, but I was reluctant to be torn from the sea and ships for a land-girt Field-Marshal. I cannot have spent all the Saturday to Monday in his company, as I did on my visit, since, whilst exploring the mill stream beyond the end of the garden and watching, fascinated, the way the trout laid up under the bank, I managed to fall in, and had to decide how best to present my dripping self at the mill. An approach by the kitchen seemed the best thing. The Field-Marshal was greatly pleased by the accident. That evening, at dinner, he asked me if I would take a glass of port. I hesitated, for form's sake; he insisted. "Bad habit; and *I* won't. But if *you* fall into the river you get a glass of port." I drank it, to the accompaniment of reflections on the talent and money dissipated in the mess, and the absurdity that there could be a right and wrong way of passing the decanters. This second stay was marked by the gift of a wrist-watch. It was a Garrard "service" model, and its clear-lined compactness (a long way from my Ingersoll pocket watch), polished brown strap smelling of good new leather, and Swiss make, all seemed consonant with the personality of its giver.

Staying with the Field-Marshal excited rather than awed me. Isington Mill contained, I considered, an impressive number of toys, though too many were under glass, fixed to the wall, or otherwise rendered inaccessible. I had the feeling of being precariously on holiday. The Field-Marshal remained too unpredictable, and actively interrogative, to seem a benevolent or an avuncular figure. At the moments when I seemed closest to him I saw something very like a boy of my own age, gleefully contemplating what mischief he might perpetrate next. Such a boy would not have been a particularly comfortable companion, since I disliked the local consequences of mischief, but the outlook was familiar. Nor could I ignore a real affection. Looking back I suppose that the Field-Marshal was lonely, but this does not make it the less remarkable that he was prepared to spend whole days keeping a boy entertained and amused. It was the boy who brought that period to its end.

I assume that the Field Marshal never learned the full story, but I am sure that the facts were irrelevant. I took things and people at their face value which made me eminently teasable. To the vast delight of those who went in for it nothing enraged me more than teasing and its oddly privileged moral position. It seemed permissible to tell a lie for the purpose of teasing. Indeed teasing was scarcely possible without lying, yet those who did this escaped being esteemed liars, and were often the fiercest in their denunciation of untruth. I was never able to work this out, and could not see that teasing was other than a perpetual taking of unjust advantage. When my school report described me as "over-solemn", I decided to abandon my ambition to be a missionary and to become a bandit instead, an ambition for which I found a warrant in Russell Thorndike's *Dr Syn*, a story by a son of the clergy, set in the country from which I came, and read to us by Richard Lewis under the cedar tree on Sunday evenings in summer. I was confirmed in my ambition by a growing sense of resentment that many of the things that other boys did or had as a matter of course could never be mine. The tally of my crimes soon involved theft, possession of dangerous weapons and regular breaking of bounds. I had a dug-out inspired by tales of the victors at Dien Bien Phu, and only desisted from sniping the occasional member of staff because they all seemed to have redeeming characteristics. (At St John's this would have been another matter.) The music mistress walked to Tanglewood unaware that only the inertia of my trigger finger interposed between her and death. I was seriously determined to be wicked; I was detected and treated with puzzlement and charity. The business must have caused embarrassment and pain to my parents, to the Lewises, and to Phyllis Reynolds, on a scale of which I can scarcely conceive. My school report, a copy of which went to the Field-Marshal, glossed the matter. But I had ceased to be a trusting child before these things occurred, and could never be a trusted child thereafter. There was no possible renegotiation of my treaties with authority. I was doomed to be suspicious, and saw (I had only to look in a mirror) furtiveness as the concomitant of suspicion.

When the Field-Marshal came to Northaw I was sent up to him, Matron or Mrs Reynolds having previously looked me over to see I was tidy. These private parades were arranged so as not to be conspicuous to other boys. Originally they were something I enjoyed. But when I faced him next it was an

Richard Luckett

ordeal that had made me miserable in anticipation, and was to continue to do so in retrospection.

By the time I reached St John's the Field-Marshal had taken to replying to my letters by returning them with a line written at the foot. In January, 1958, however, he had been unexpectedly expansive, perhaps because of the size of his Trianon Palace Hotel notepaper:

> Thank you for your letter. I am glad you have had a good holiday. I imagine you are now back at Northaw so I am addressing this letter there. I am off tonight to Austria for a week and then go to Switzerland for a month – to get away from all the fog and bad weather of England and Paris.
>
> Yours sincerely,
> Montgomery of Alamein

I noted the omission of love and was unaware that the weather in England was bad. It was after this that my letters started to boomerang. It now seems unsurprising. Everybody was moving; he (though I didn't know this) into retirement, my parents to a new parish at Lyminge, I to my new school. My dutiful letters continued, but they were poor, evasive things. I could not tell him that I hated this place over which he Olympianly presided, and which he knew nothing about.

The inspections continued. They were conducted with a bouncy jocularity which became much more pronounced when a new and young headmaster (Montgomery's personal appointment, we understood) took over from Hereward Wake who had had about him a *gravitas* that awed us greatly and perhaps even subdued the Field-Marshal. "Ah, Headmaster," he would now begin, "this is Luckett. Do you beat him often?" The headmaster, thank heaven, did not, but my fear that he might was intensified by the certitude that the Field-Marshal would be approving if he had. The

Field-Marshal did concern himself with aspects of my school career other than socially acceptable naughtiness; the last letter that I have from him, in August, 1960, runs:

> Thank you for your letter; I am glad to learn that you are settling down in your new home.
>
> I was interesting (*sic*) to see you receive several prizes last term, which is very good. I hope you will do equally well at the prize giving next year.

The shaky syntax now reminds me sharply that the Field-Marshal was 72 when he wrote it – not something that I thought of at the time.

Montgomery's slackening of interest did not prevent him remaining, so far as I was concerned, the ferret at the rabbit-hole of life. Life in its Johnian aspect I did not in any case care for. The library was an essential refuge, but even there he inexorably impinged. By persuading a benefactor to give to the school a new chapel he made possible the conversion of the old one into a new library; his interest extended to the frequent gift of boxes of books, which as a librarian I often had to catalogue. These boxes were generally of cullings from his recent reading, usually bought from Hugh Rees of Pall Mall, and they might have mitigated my feeling towards him had I ever reflected on their nature. He certainly bought and read everything written by Robert Graves, and also by C. Day Lewis. On the other hand he did not keep these books.

If I did (it cannot have been conscious) discern some common ground here, my manner of exploring it invited disaster. In the early and trusting days the Field-Marshal had repeatedly said: "If you ever want anything, ask me, and I will give it you." I had been taught not to ask. When I finally did so it was because books had become my life. An exhibition of Penguins in the Library exhausted my pocket money and made me long for the purchases I could not make. I remembered the Field-Marshal's injunction, summoned up my courage, and wrote and asked for money to buy paperbacks. In particular I wanted the Penguin Swinburne, Jeffares on Yeats, and a book on Dylan Thomas. For several days I awaited the delivery of post at breakfast with a trepidation that in itself told me I had done the wrong thing. Nothing came. Then my housemaster, Derek Pitt, summoned me to his study. He had before him, all too evidently, my letter to the Field-Marshal.

Derek was a kindly man from whom I learnt much history, and whom I eventually got to know well. He was new to his job as housemaster, and much perplexed. I had distressed the Field-Marshal by my importunity. Why had I done this? I explained as best I could. A difficult but friendly interview concluded with my promise to write a letter of apology, and Derek's thrusting at me a couple of pound notes that I knew to have come from him. I bought the books. But I trembled at the thought of encountering Montgomery again.

I was bound to do so, and the circumstances could not have been more difficult. At St John's membership of the Corps was compulsory, and the Corps seemed to me the quintessence of everything dislikeable about this place that I so disliked. Khaki and blanco distilled the essence of the dirty changing rooms and foul bathrooms and latrines; drill the mindlessness of the team spirit, and drill was, besides, the indice of "attitude" – an offence that might lead to a house prefects' beating, each prefect allowed his crack of the cane. It was all palpably futile and wasteful. But I had noticed that the Corps mindlessness was institutionalized. It was considered, administratively, a quite separate entity from the school. It was not, that is to say, constructed with reference to the school lists, nor did it even maintain its cadres from year to year. Rather, it was re-embodied out of a general muster at the beginning of each. This commencement parade was always a notably grizzly and protracted experience. It occurred to me that if I failed to turn up at it I should simply cease to exist so far as the Corps was concerned. I put my theory to the test as soon as the calendar permitted; to my immense gratification the theory was vindicated.

The afternoons thus liberated (by a lesson learned from Gogol) I spent in the pleasing seclusion of the library office, doing a little card-indexing to quieten my conscience when it troubled me and reading books (often the Field-Marshal's gifts) when, as was the case for the greatest part of the time, I was more struck by my own good sense in achieving this freedom. It was when I gathered that the Field-Marshal was coming to inspect the Corps that I realized that, while it was easy to become disembodied, ghosts who needed to get back on strength had a far harder problem to resolve.

I was fortunate in grasping the essential pomposity of those masters who officered the Corps – the only insight into human nature ever afforded me by the works (a compulsory affliction) of Gilbert and Sullivan. It dawned on me that I had no better tactic than to make an (almost) clean breast of it. I therefore had myself marched into the orderly room by RSM Joad at a time when the Officer Commanding was in attendance. I explained my predicament, saying no more than that I had been left off the lists for eighteen months. In what proportions fear of ridicule and essential benevolence mingled in the reception with which this plea was greeted I cannot tell; my guess is about half and half. But I was there when the Corps was duly inspected, and for nothing. The Field-Marshal cast his eye over me and passed me by. I was not in the least convinced that, had I not been there, he would have noticed my absence.

My last year at St John's was surprisingly enjoyable. I became a school prefect and head of house and allowed canings and the informer system to fall into desuetude. But the Field-Marshal took no interest in these implausible elevations. Perversely, I began to take an interest in him.

Richard Luckett

Corelli Barnett's *The Desert Generals* had appeared in 1960; it was not resoundingly publicized at St John's. I borrowed it from Leatherhead Public Library and read it with intense enjoyment. It immediately dispelled that feeling of oppression which the Field-Marshal's myth had long induced in me.

Despite this I was not convinced by the book, and in consequence I began to read up the desert campaigns and to develop an interest in military history. My reaction also made me aware of the extent to which, through no fault of his, I had found the fact of the Field-Marshal's generosity burdensome. Both these tendencies persisted after I had left St John's and gone to Cambridge, where I spent three happy years reading (occasionally for the English Tripos) and producing opera. At the end of that time I had no clear notion as to what I wished to do; the occupations that I hoped to follow I dared not, as they seemed unlikely to provide a living, and a damaged leg (a consequence, after having first seen *La Boutique Fantasque*, of a manic urge to imitate Nureyev) intensified my natural caution. And in a stronger way three years of freedom from a quotidian sense of obligation made an ultimate awareness of obligation more, rather than less, intense. This sense certainly played some part in my decision to take a teaching post at the RMA Sandhurst, where one of my colleagues was the Field-Marshal's stepson, John Carver, and where, as in the rest of my life for (three years aside) the previous sixteen years, the Field-Marshal might at any day appear.

He did. Rumour had it that he had changed, but I could not discern how. His head moved with that same downwards sweep to the right when he asked questions, then snapped back to centre, eyes riveted and riveting. His enquiries were as terse as ever. Officers of field rank, I suddenly realized, were not, to him, distinguishable from small boys. I was twice introduced to him in the mess (where, as we assembled, a colleague encouraged me by murmuring in my ear: "Such a very good suit, Richard; pity it wasn't made for you"). He held court in front of the fire. On both occasions we talked. They were interrogations I had had before, even become adept at by now. On neither occasion was there the slightest indication that he had recognized me.

Monty the Author

Alan Howarth

ALAN HOWARTH CBE MP *was born in 1944. He was Senior Research Assistant for Montgomery's* History of Warfare *1966–1967. He taught at Westminster School from 1968–1974 and was Personal Assistant to the Chairman of the Conservative Party 1975–1979, Director of the Conservative Research Department 1979–1981 and Vice-Chairman of the Party 1980–1981. He then joined Baring Brothers. Since 1983 he has been MP for Stratford-upon-Avon.*

MY EARLIEST MEMORY of the Field-Marshal (as he was always known in our family) goes back to when I was four years old, sitting on his knee and eating Fuller's walnut cake as a consolation for having been unable to count up all the medals on his battledress. From time to time in my childhood he would appear in my parents' home. Each visitation was an impressive occasion though not a daunting one. The force of his personality was mitigated by the accompanying present of Toblerone or Turkish Delight and of course by his twinkle and playfulness.

As a sixteen-year-old schoolboy I took it upon myself, when I was working for a prize essay on "The Problems of Central Africa", to write and ask him for his thoughts. This was the response:

Isington Mill
27-2-61

My dear Alan,

I have just returned from six weeks in Switzerland and was delighted to hear from you. I regard you as one of my young friends and the fact that you wrote to me shows that you want to be so regarded – and I am glad.

You ask me about a terrific problem. I am just off to London for two days; when I return I will see what I can do for you; I will try and get some ideas to you by Monday morning next.

I expect that as the term draws to an end you begin to

feel the financial wind. Here is a small present (10/-) which may help to keep the wolf from the door.

I hope you will visit me again in your Easter holidays so that we can have a good talk about things. Let me know when you would like to come.

Yrs sincerely,
Montgomery of Alamein

In 1964 George Rainbird and John Hadfield, with characteristic publishing flair, had the idea of commissioning Montgomery to write a history of warfare. The Field-Marshal sought advice from my father, an historian and headmaster, as to how he should recruit his research team, and my father steered the opportunity in my direction. Apart from the intrinsic interest of the project, the terms proposed were startlingly generous. I would have a research colleague (whom I would select), a secretary, a flat with all expenses met and a fee of £2,000 a year. To a third year undergraduate reading history and with no certain ideas about his future it was a proposition not lightly to be dismissed. My Cambridge tutors and supervisors were horrified, of course. Monty would at no stage have appealed to the luxurious minds of King's, but in the mid-sixties – when Harold Wilson had just formed his first administration, when Roy Jenkins and the *Guardian* were setting the moral tone and the *New Left Review* was *de rigueur* on every academic coffee table – Monty was derisorily out of fashion. Nevertheless, I took the job, and a great deal of instruction, amusement and happiness followed for me.

The Field-Marshal's own enthusiasm and conviction of the value of the project upon which we were embarking were exhilarating from the start. So was his total confidence in my colleague, Anthony Wainwright, and myself. His famous capacity to take the major decisions and then to delegate what did not require his personal attention were quickly evinced.

In the early months of 1965, as soon as he had recuperated from a prostate operation, he drafted six short, reflective chapters. These, which eventually became the first two and the last four chapters of the book, were for the guidance of the research team. The next stage of the operation entailed Anthony and me arriving for lunch at Claridge's with a proposed table of contents. The table of contents was approved over snails and champagne.

Thereafter the Field-Marshal set deadlines for the completion of each chapter, and held us relentlessly to the programme. In his words there were "no set office hours or trade union rules". In twenty-one months we covered the history of warfare from Sargon, priest of Ishtar, to Montgomery himself.

In the early months there were some hiccups in the schedule. But so formidable was the Field-Marshal's displeasure that we soon hiccuped no more. Typically we would deliver a draft chapter, late on the eve of the date it fell due, at Mount Pleasant Post Office (and then repair to the New Friends Chinese Restaurant in Salmon Lane with a glorious sensation of relief). The Field-Marshal stipulated that the draft material should be typed in double-spacing, each paragraph starting on a new sheet. He would spend a few days preparing the "red ink version". We would then go and stay the following weekend in his home at Isington Mill to discuss and finalize the text.

The sessions I had with the Field-Marshal over those drafts were as formative as any part of my education. It was then that I learned to appreciate his distinctive qualities of mind: his extraordinary self-discipline and power of concentration, his ability to discern the essential amid the mass of detail, his capacity for fruitful simplification. I also observed the pleasure he took in the precise and telling use of words – I had been aware of this of course from reading in his *Memoirs* his immensely moving messages to the Eighth Army. In these negotiations over our text I learned a great deal myself about how to distinguish the essential from the inessential, how to negotiate, and how to pursue my objective with determination and tact. He was a tough bargainer, but he would always listen; he was never overbearing or impatient; and he made me feel I was doing my job properly if I said what I thought was right. At the end of the project, when we were correcting the galley-proofs, he wrote to me with tongue-in-cheek pedantry:

> We must clear up the matter of "cooperation" and "co-ordination".
> *I agree "cooperation"*
> Regarding the other. In Galley 1 of Chapter 1, under Grand Strategy, it is spelt *co*-ordination – which I consider right. Similarly in Chapter 3, Galley 7, line 17. Lower down in Galley 7, Chapter 3, it is spelt "coordination".
> I stand for "co-ordination", *vide* Concise Oxford Dictionary.
> I will *not* give way on this.
> Get it cleared up by Wednesday.

I myself did not always show his forebearance and when after about six months I wrote to him grumbling about something or other this was his response:

> Isington Mill
> 30-1-66
>
> My dear Alan,
> 1. Chapter 8, delivered after the birth pangs of London and Bournemouth, duly arrived here first post yesterday. It covers a difficult period and you have tackled it splendidly. I congratulate you.
> 2. I am sorry you should have thought it necessary to write as you did in the second para of your note dated

28 January. We are engaged on a cooperative effort. I am very old; you are very young. When age and youth combine there are bound to be differences in points of view, and occasional clashes; indeed what surprises me is that we have had so few. You probably consider me to be very irritating at times; maybe I have certain views on that subject myself!

Anyhow, if I have hurt your feelings, of course I apologise; indeed that is the last thing I would ever want to do.

3. You are engaged in what is probably the biggest thing in your life, because of what can follow. If we pull this off, your future is assured. My main preoccupation (apart from the book) is to ensure that when our task is completed you and Anthony are put securely on the way to higher things, and that matter occupies my thoughts daily – and will continue to do so, come what may.

4. I suggest we have a quiet talk about things on Tuesday evening next, when you arrive here to discuss Chapter 8.

We are exactly halfway though the book, having completed 13 chapters out of 26; I wrote six chapters myself, unaided, before you two began work on it.

I reckoned some small celebration was needed so I have ordered my new Belgian cook to lay on a *spécialité* dinner; it would be a pity to ruin it by differences of viewpoints. So can you arrive here by 6.30 p.m., so that we can sort things out before dinner?

Do not forget the rush-hour traffic.

5. I attach some thoughts on a lead-in for Chapter 7.

6. I have received the tickets for England v Ireland at Twickenham on 12 Feb., and will give you yours on Tuesday.

Yrs ever
Montgomery of Alamein

The Field-Marshal's generosity and his capacity to encourage colleagues who were little more than a quarter of his age are characteristically evident in a letter he wrote to me in October, 1966: "It seems clear that you have taught me to become a minor sort of historian! I hope I may have taught you to understand a bit about soldiering!!"

He was immensely hospitable at Isington Mill, and his reputation as martinet and teetotaller was altogether at odds with the reality of his gifts as a host. Just as he had insisted that Anthony and I should be comfortably accommodated in London, so when we stayed with him we were treated with great consideration and generosity. We had breakfast in bed, although this practice was discontinued after Anthony one morning knocked his tray off the bedside table. In the first year of our endeavours the claret he offered his guests was Château Lafite 1952; thereafter we had to make do with the 1958 vintage ("£2 a bottle", as he liked to remind us). He enjoyed serving the wine, even if a purist might have deplored the placing of the decanter beside the radiator. If white wine was required he produced champagne – on one occasion a 1947 Lanson – and he insisted on the activation of a twizzle-stick. Before dinner there was Tio Pepe and after dinner, in case it should be supposed that life at Isington Mill was all sophistication, cherry brandy. The Field-Marshal would eat very little himself and of course drank water, but as the evening wore on he became mellow at the same pace as we did.

The Field-Marshal demanded our absolute commitment. A suggestion that a skiing holiday might refresh body and mind was strongly rejected in an interview at the Athenaeum. That our London flat was at 2 Hyde Park Place over George Rainbird's offices was in a way a symbol of our being on duty twenty-four hours a day. Although in reality he knew and enjoyed the fact that we amused ourselves very considerably in London, deference was always paid to the notion that life was solid work: "Without great toil those who succeed are few."

In return for our commitment his loyalty to us was total –
and fierce. At the end of 1966 the Rainbird publishing firm
moved to new offices and it was necessary to find another flat.
One of the senior staff at Rainbird dared to question whether
it was appropriate for us to occupy a very pleasant furnished
flat in South Kensington at 26 guineas a week. The Field-
Marshal wrote to George Rainbird: "Will you please inject
some commonsense into your staff before they have a head-
on collision with me – which is imminent. . . . It is not
possible to get the type of flat they need at less than 26
guineas a week for a short let; it would be more like 30
guineas. The book is now at a very critical stage. We are
working up to the major conflicts of the 20th century. I am
not prepared to have my research team mucked about by
your staff at this stage in the battle. I cannot understand
bellyaching at this stage about a few pounds – over the
finishing of a book which will sell a million copies."

When that particular battle had been fought, he wrote to
me: "I am not standing any nonsense when it comes to what I
consider is right and proper for you two lads. . . . The great
thing is that he has capitulated. Meanwhile I suggest you
forget all about it, get on with the work – and walk delicately,
like Agag!" I can only say that George Rainbird and his staff
were amazingly forbearing.

Another person who was seen off in a spirit of aggressive
loyalty to us was Captain Stephen Roskill, the distinguished
naval historian and biographer of Lord Hankey. Roskill had
encouraged me in my last year at Cambridge to do academic
research and had made strenuous efforts to dissuade me from
working with the Field-Marshal. Later, while I was working
on *A History of Warfare*, he asked me when that project was
completed to be his research assistant on his biography of
Hankey, which I declined to do. When *A History of Warfare*
was published in 1968 Roskill wrote a fairly tart review.
Monty rounded on him, quoting a letter he had sent after

receiving an advance copy of the book: "I truly found it absolutely enthralling, and above all a masterpiece of lucidity and compression". The next day the Field-Marshal wrote to me:

Isington Mill
24-9-68

My dear Alan,

I received from Roskill this morning an abject apology for his criticisms of my research team, and of your research in particular. He looked up a number of books and found you were right, generally. He ended by saying "I should have checked before writing".

I have thanked him for his generous apology.

Yrs ever,

M of A

Other reviews of the finished work were very kind. Michael Howard wrote in the *Sunday Times*: "Even if Lord Montgomery did give his research assistants a fairly free rein, the final result has all the clarity, precision and vigour that one would expect from any book bearing his imprimatur. With the aid of the Lord Mighty in Battle, the Field-Marshal has once more hit them for six." The reviewer in *The Times Literary Supplement* wrote: "Lord Montgomery's stimulating book must surely take its place as a classic commentary on the history of warfare. . . . That it is permeated with his particular and well remembered idiosyncracies, the freshness and vigour of his approach to any subject, will only enhance its undoubted value as a deeply interesting, often inspiring and intensely instructive book."

A Foyle's Luncheon was held on 1st October, 1968, with A. J. P. Taylor in the chair and among the guests Field-Marshal Lord Slim and Field-Marshal Sir Gerald Templer. Afterwards Monty wrote to me, "I had to sign 150 copies of the book, all bought and paid for in the room! Over 100 copies were sold at London Airport on the day of publication – September 30th." And more disingenuously, "I am fed up with all the publicity. My post every morning is enormous. I may soon go mad!"

The book has remained in some demand since then. In 1971 I produced an abridged version, two-thirds the length of the original, for a new edition, and in 1982 the original version was reprinted in an edition by Janes.

The Field-Marshal's loyalty was not of the kind that would expire with one's contract of employment. He had always shown a fatherly concern that Anthony Wainwright and I should not sow disproportionate quantities of wild oats, that we should be launched on sensible career paths and that we should marry nice girls.

In 1966 I met Gillie Chance whom, after a courtship both monitored and promoted by the Field-Marshal, I married the following year. It pleased the Field-Marshal with his own Irish blood that Gillie was Irish and at an early stage I received the following letter:

Isington Mill
6-11-66

My dear Alan,

The Irish Lunch
Thursday, November 10
I will be at Claridge's, usual seat, at about 12.10 p.m.
I suggest you and your Irish lady arrive 12.15 p.m.
Anthony and his selected lady to arrive say 5 minutes after you. We will lunch at 12.30.
I have to get to the House of Lords at 2.30 p.m. Southern Rhodesia is to be debated and there may be quite a hulla-baloo!

Yrs ever,
Montgomery of Alamein
P.S. Have you found a flat to which to move?

In January, 1967, as had become his wont at that season of the year, the Field-Marshal went to stay for a month in a hotel in Bournemouth. He installed his research team with him. It was a massively chintzy hotel, the average age of the residents being about the same as the Field-Marshal's and service distinguished only by the fact that milk puddings were available at all hours. It was not a place that appealed to me, and this tended to reflect itself in a mood in me which the Field-Marshal termed "the pip". Various remedies were tried. Touchingly one evening the Field-Marshal pressed into my hand a prayer book. As that did not prove immediately efficacious, the next day at lunch he had a telephone brought to the table and summoned Gillie to Bournemouth forthwith. The following morning I was ordered to work in my room and on no account to wander around. It was, again, touching to see from my window Gillie on the Field-Marshal's arm as they walked up and down the sea front sniffing the "ozone" which he insisted was the restorative feature of Bournemouth in January.

After Gillie and I had both returned to London the Field-Marshal wrote to me:

Isington Mill
24-1-67

My dear Alan,

I have sent Gillie a copy of my *Memoirs*, the expensive edition and not a paper-back! You might see that she reads it. I have inscribed it:

"With love, from . . ."

I hope that is all right by you!!

Thank you for your nice "Bournemouth" letter. I always enjoy being with you. I do worry about you sometimes – not the ordinary type of worry because I never really worry about anything, and certainly not in my everyday life. But during our close association over the book we are writing, I have developed a great affection for you and it upsets me when you are unhappy. I think the right word is "upset", not worry. Whatever the future may hold for you, you can count on my help and backing and I cannot say more than that. I always think we are sent into this world to be happy and to create happiness for others. But some of us need help. Whenever you feel in need of help, or inner strength, come and unburden your soul to me. You will never come in vain: that I can promise.

Yrs always,
Montgomery of Alamein

He continued to encourage the course of true love or, as he put it, "push at the back of the scrum". Gillie and I duly became engaged to be married and went to see the Field-Marshal one day in July. After our visit he wrote:

Isington Mill
23-7-67

My dear Alan,

It was good of you to write as you did after you and Gillie had come here on Wednesday, July 19. It is exactly right that you should marry Gillie. When you came in from the garden, where I had sent you, I had just finished handing you over to her – in much the same way that I commended you to her father.

Life can be a bit of a struggle at times, as I know very well. Whenever you are in want of help, or advice, you will *both* always find a warm welcome waiting for you here. And you can come and stay here whenever you want to get away from London. Just ask yourselves. I do not see myself undertaking any new project, as you suggest may happen. I propose to enjoy myself, and to help others who may not be so fortunate to do the same.

Yrs ever,
Montgomery of Alamein

169

Alan Howarth

We were married in Dublin in September and the Field-Marshal came over for the wedding – his first visit to Southern Ireland since active service in County Cork in the early 1920s (which he said was the most unpleasant military operation with which he was ever involved). He treated the organization of this expedition as if it were a latter-day Normandy landing. "Where are my maps of Dublin and surrounding country: with marriage site clearly marked?"

Over the next three years or so, until he entered his last, long decline, the Field-Marshal invited Gillie and me frequently to Isington Mill and each winter to Bournemouth. Latterly he compartmentalized his friendships less than before and at Bournemouth in particular there were lunches with other people whose company he particularly enjoyed: the Liddell Harts (though he would sometimes complain that "Basil talks like a machine-gun"), Bernard Levin, the de Fonblanques. I picture him enraptured with amusement holding a napkin up to his eyes as he laughed, until his mischievous face reappeared with his eyes puckered as he delivered his story in staccato bursts interrupted by giggles.

His humour was very much a matter of self-mockery, a parody of the style which he knew was attributed to him. At the Bournemouth hotel he would observe to the Italian waiters that they were lucky to be alive. "Anthony has had his hair cut three times during the last month!!", he wrote when inviting Gillie and me to Isington Mill with Anthony Wainwright. Another time when we were invited down for the day he wrote to assure us "It will be fine! I will give orders!!" Writing from Bournemouth to correct an uncharacteristic slip of the pen he said, "If in a later letter I said March 1st, it must be that I am going mad – arguing with Basil Liddell Hart, or maybe the ozone has been too much for my brain!"

In the authentic British military tradition the French nation presented to him a field full of amusement. When he was about to disagree with some proposition he would open with a flamboyant *"Malheureusement . . ."*, in imitation of his French staff in past times. "Anthony is coming to lunch – *seul, pas de bêtises avec Claudia"* (whom, with Monty's lively support, he would in due course marry). He enjoyed tags of songs and rhymes in French, such as this:

> *Mademoiselle Fifi le Bon-Bon*
> *Fut attrapée avec son pantalon en bas.*
> *Tout le monde s'écrie,*
> *"Quelle miséricorde, quel dommage".*

One day, after he had encouraged Gillie to talk about the school at which she was teaching, he appeared having composed a telegram to the Head Mistress:

> I have heard a great deal about you from Mrs Howarth – not all good. I am an old widower; you are a spinster of uncertain age; obviously we have much in common; we must meet. Je suis triste. Honi soit qui mal y pense. Quel misericorde quel domage (sic). I have a nice house, and beaucoup d'argent. A second telegram follows. Tout à vous. Field-Marshal Montgomery of Alamein.

Though never really indelicate he was certainly neither prim nor intolerant. He once mentioned as a dark secret an escapade of his own as a young man in a *maison* in Arthur Road, Bombay. He described a disagreement that he had had with Auchinleck in Southern Command when Auchinleck had ordered that every soldier should at all times carry his rifle. Monty had disagreed – "bellyached" – on the grounds that consideration should be had for the interests of "a soldier who walks out in the gloaming with some girl or buys six pennyworth of dark in the cinema to do a bit of necking". He recalled that he had been beaten by the High Master of St Paul's, Walker, for circulating a rhyme about Uriah the Hittite:

David on his palace roof
In his night attire
Saw a lady in her bath;
Her name was Mrs Uriah.

He sent a letter to the battle:
"If you would be saved
Put Uriah in the line of fire –
Yours sincerely, David."

The Old Testament provided a rich seam of humour in his self-parodying mode. Death he commonly referred to as "going over Jordan". On an occasion when for some reason I observed that Victor Hugo at the age of 80 had become the father of a child the Field-Marshal trumped that by observing that Abraham had done as much at 104. When Anthony Wainwright and I had finished our work on *A History of Warfare* we gave the Field-Marshal a present of a West African grey parrot (which he had said was what he would really like), and he called the parrot Moses. (Sadly the parrot died after a week – an event which the Field-Marshal insisted should not be revealed to Gillie so as not to upset her).

The Field-Marshal's table talk was little about politics – "a rough and dirty game" – but a certain amount about politicians. He was largely charitable in his comments – though he did once say that since the Garter was an Order of Chivalry Harold Macmillan would certainly never qualify. He did not like to be taken for granted as a Conservative, and mentioned quite typically in a letter in September, 1965, that "Both parties are angling for my attendance as much as possible in the House of Lords in what is going to be a very turbulent session – the Conservatives because I take the Tory Whip, the Labour Party because they reckon I can help them in some issues (which I can)." He said he regarded the possession of money as a stewardship and that this was something the Socialists understood better than the Conservatives.

He had a photograph of himself with Ernie Bevin hung in his sitting room and told a story to illustrate why he had liked Bevin very much. Attending a Labour Cabinet meeting as Chief of the Imperial General Staff he had argued that it was necessary to attract more public school boys into the post-war army.

> Gaiskell: "That's not democratic."
> Montgomery: "I reckon I know better than you do what's democratic. You went to a very expensive public school. I went to a London day school, and I've never had a penny that I didn't earn by the sweat of my brow."
> Bevin: " 'ear, 'ear."

He recalled that of three Secretaries of State for War with whom he had worked closely Mannie Shinwell was easily the best. Two things were required of a Secretary of State: he must understand and he must make decisions. The first Secretary of State he dealt with could do neither. The second could not understand but wanted to make decisions. "Finally I went to Attlee and said to him we can't go on with this, and he gave me Shinwell – who would fight for you."

He regarded Lloyd George (whom he had heard address a public meeting in Welsh) and Churchill as the two political geniuses of his lifetime – though it intrigued him that Churchill had said to him that the ablest man he had known in British politics was A. J. Balfour. Churchill, he always insisted, was "the greatest of my friends". He said that Churchill had been "like a cat on a hot tin roof before the battle of Alamein – the rats were getting at him". But his loyalty to Churchill was total, and he was immensely fond of

Lady Churchill. He had much to say in praise of contemporary Conservative politicians: Heath, Whitelaw, Carrington. He thought that Enoch Powell would one day be Prime Minister.

Of his military colleagues the only one of whom he ever spoke to me with acerbity was Lord Tedder. He had a particularly high admiration for Slim. Of the Generals who served under him, he said that Dempsey was the only "grand chef". He was probably fondest of Oliver Leese.

Tycoons interested him very much and it is easy to imagine that with his childhood insecurity, his single-mindedness and his will to power he could have become one himself if he had not chosen to be a soldier. He counted among his friends Anton Rupert, Garfield Weston and Roy Thomson.

He loved to talk about his family and his particular friends, but in my experience he kept them apart. I never met his son, David, until after the Field-Marshal had died. He was loyal to his family, but one of his childhood recollections is instructive about his psychological formation. As a boy he was caught smoking. His father took him to the chapel where they prayed together, after which his father told him he was forgiven. As they came out of the chapel his mother was waiting with the cane.

I once asked the Field-Marshal what he valued most in life. He replied, "I have the grand cross of every order in Europe. But you asked me what I value most. What I value most is the affection of the soldiers who fought with me. I stopped in my car at the lights at the bottom of Whitehall the other day, and a bus driver leant out of his cab and said 'Hallo Monty!' That's what I value most."

In Memoriam

John Harding

FIELD-MARSHAL LORD HARDING OF PETHERTON, GCB, CBE, MC *was born in 1896 and served with the Machine Gun Corps in the First World War. In the Second World War he commanded the Seventh Armoured Division until he was wounded in the battle for Tripoli and was later Chief of Staff to General Alexander. He was Chief of the Imperial General Staff from 1952–1955 and Governor and Commander-in-Chief in Cyprus from 1955–1957.*

Sandhurst Chapel, Sunday, 30 October, 1977

I COUNT IT A great honour to have been invited to give the address at this service of dedication for the unveiling of a memorial window to the late Field-Marshal The Viscount Montgomery of Alamein, universally known as "Monty" affectionately by his troops, respectfully by his enemies. It is as "Monty" that I shall refer to him through the rest of this address.

This is an address not a sermon – all the same I have found it useful on such occasions to have a text, and the text I have chosen for this address is some words from verse 53 of the 78th Psalm; they read –

". . . and he led them on safely so that they feared not."

I had the good fortune to know Monty as a teacher at the Staff College, as a commander in battle, as the professional head of the Army in the office of CIGS, and most important of all to me, as a friend.

He was a brilliant teacher – he never left you in the air or in doubt. His lectures were concise and crystal clear. I have vivid recollections of one occasion when I was the spokesman for my syndicate on a tactical exercise. I started to give my answer to the first problem, full of confidence in the merits of our solution. I hadn't gone far when Monty stopped me, asking, "You would do so and so would you – that's interesting – continue." That was the first warning shot. I continued, to be stopped with the comment, "Now, that's very interesting."

Then I knew I was in trouble; but he let me finish and then said, "Well Harding, your syndicate's solution is very interesting but in my view it could have only one result – a scene of intense military confusion." But he didn't leave it at that; he proceeded to give us, in clear and simple terms, his own solution, which we all had to admit was sound and would certainly not have resulted in "a scene of intense military confusion".

As a commander in battle he had an uncanny knack of reducing a problem to its simplest proportions, of concentrating on the essentials and cutting out the frills and furbelows. He understood the supreme importance of the morale of the soldier, and was at pains to make sure that everyone under his command, from his corps commanders down to the private soldiers, knew what was required of them, what they had to do and why. He studied his enemies, the character of their commanders, their tactics, their strengths and their weaknesses. He refused to be hurried, to attack before he was ready – he was determined "to lead us on *safely*" and in that he was ably supported and protected by General Alexander.

When he took over command in the desert he revitalised the 8th Army, restored its morale and confidence, made sure all was ready before he launched us into the attack. Then he led us on safely and he led us to victory.

There were those who claimed that he was self-centred, that he was devoid of compassion. I totally disagree and let me tell you why. Early in 1943 during the pursuit from Alamein to Tripoli, I had the misfortune to get in the way of a salvo from a German 105 battery. Fortunately for myself I survived, thanks mainly to the arrangements for my rapid evacuation to hospital made by my senior staff officer, now a Field-Marshal, who I am very glad is also here today to pay tribute to Monty. Some months later, when I was still in hospital outside Cairo, I got a message to say Monty was coming to see me. I knew he must be very busy and I expected a short visit. Not a bit of it. He pulled up a chair by my bed, sent his ADC away and spent an hour or more telling me all that had happened since I was wounded, particularly the exploits of my old division, and of his plans for my future. At that time the doctors had written off my chances of further active duty and Monty knew it. I shall always remember with deep gratitude that act of kindness and compassion. He knew he had nothing to gain from me.

Having completed the defeat of the German forces in North-West Europe, and having set the stage for the occupation, Monty took over the post of Chief of the Imperial General Staff, the professional head of the Army, in June, 1946. This was a particularly difficult time. The run-down of the Army from a war footing to peacetime conditions, but with many continuing commitments in all parts of the world, had created new and complex problems. I was one of his senior commanders at the time and I was thankful to have a man with his experience and knowledge, his courage and foresight, at the head of the Army's affairs. To me he remained as accessible and resolute as I had known him in battle. He was always ready to listen and respond to argument based on common sense and reason. After his tour of duty as CIGS he went to Western Union and then NATO, where he played a most important part in the organization, training and efficiency of the armed forces of NATO on which we in this country mainly depend for our security. After his retirement he continued to take the closest personal interest in the efficiency and well-being of the Army. He never failed to use his powerful position of influence in what he believed to be its best interests.

I am not suggesting that he was infallible or that he was perfect. He wouldn't have been human if he had been. With the advantage of hindsight it can fairly be said that he made some mistakes – but they were few, very few.

There were some at the time, and there are more now who

write books and so on, who think they could have done better. For my part I am thankful they weren't given the chance to try. His son, his grandchildren and other members of his family, have every reason to be intensely proud of his life and his achievements in the service of our country. He belongs to that select and illustrious company of

> Brave men, and worthy patriots,
> dear to God and famous to all ages.

To sum it all up Monty was a professional soldier of the highest quality. From the time he was a cadet here at Sandhurst he devoted himself to the study of his profession and the conduct of war, to the development of his qualifications for high command. As a commander in battle he ranks with Marlborough and Wellington, as a leader he had the inspiration of Nelson. He was a trusted comrade in arms and a firm friend.

And now I would like to conclude by addressing a few words specifically to the cadets here today and to succeeding generations of cadets who will follow you. When you come to this chapel and look up at that window which has just been unveiled, remember firstly that it commemorates a great soldier, whose life and achievements it will repay you to study; and secondly that it commemorates a great leader, who will always be remembered and honoured in the hearts and minds of all those like myself who had the privilege of serving under his command in battle as the man who "led us on safely so that we feared not".